PREPARING ADMINISTRATORS: NEW PERSPECTIVES

Edited by

Jack A. Culbertson

Stephen P. Hencley

UNIVERSITY COUNCIL FOR EDUCATIONAL ADMINISTRATION

65 South Oval Drive

Columbus 10, Ohio

Acknowledgments

The editors wish to express their appreciation for the support, assistance, and co-operation which made possible the publication of this volume. First, to the Fund for the Advancement of Education, Ford Foundation, for its support of the national conference on "Preparing Administrators: New Perspectives" held in Chicago, October 16-18, 1961. The support received from the Fund made possible activities of substantial importance to the development of this book: the development of ten papers outlining new perspectives for pre-service and in-service preparation of school administrators; the opportunity to discuss initial drafts of eight of these papers with selected UCEA professors at a two-day pre-conference meeting; the opportunity for ample consideration and discussion of the papers at the three-day national conference held in Chicago; the opportunity to bring the ideas contained in this volume to the attention of a much wider audience in their present published form.

Appreciation is expressed to a number of persons who assisted the contributing authors in sharpening the focus of their papers during the pre-conference meeting held in July, 1961: Howard Bretsch, University of Michigan; John Guy Fowlkes, University of Wisconsin; Daniel E. Griffiths, New York University; Meno Lovenstein, Ohio State University; Sidney P. Marland, Superintendent of Schools, Winnetka, Illinois; Roderick McPhee, Harvard University; Leon Osview, Temple University; John Ramseyer, Ohio State University.

Finally, appreciation is expressed to the writers who developed papers for presentation at the national conference on "Preparing Administrators: New Perspectives": A. D. Albright, University of Kentucky; James Harlow, University of Oklahoma; Dan Lortie, Harvard University; John Millett, Miami University; Theodore Reller, University of California, Berkeley; John Walton, Johns Hopkins University; Egbert Wengert, University of Oregon;. Benjamin Willis, General Superintendent of Schools, Chicago, Illinois.

J.A.C.
S.P.H.

Table of Contents

Chapter I

Forces Shaping the New Perspectives[1]

STEPHEN P. HENCLEY
University Council for
Educational Administration

Education in this country is entering a dynamic era: an era in which past traditions may become guides of strictly limited value. The emerging picture is one of change. The increasingly open confrontation of the old with the new is bringing little tranquility to those in positions of educational leadership and even less opportunity to cling to the anchor of the familiar.

The dimensions of change exerting influence on the goals, character, and direction of American education have many sources:

Satellite competition, cold wars, and world-wide ideological conflicts are continuing to reaffirm the important role of education in the affairs of men. The precariousness of the world situation, the clash of conflicting value systems, the competition of aggressive nations in the space race, and the necessity of marshalling total resources in the interest of survival have all dramatically highlighted the crucial role that national scholarship plays in the destiny of nations. A significant twentieth century phenomenon is world-wide recognition of education as a tremendous national resource.

The current population "explosion," the increased mobility of the American population, and the phenomenal growth of metropolitanism are generating unusual educational prob-

---

[1] Some of these forces have been discussed by the writer in an introduction to the Report of the UCEA Committee entitled, "Improving Preparatory Programs for Educational Administrators in the United States: Some Action Guides." (Columbus, Ohio: University Council for Educational Administration), pp. 1-3. (Mimeographed).

1

lems. The growth of world population in this century has exhibited startling dimensions. Not only has the globe's population doubled since 1900, but also it is presently increasing at the rate of 50 million per year. Estimates indicate that the current world population of 3 billion will more than double again in the next forty years. If present world living standards are to be maintained, it will be necessary for nations of the world not only to double their capital investments by the year 2000, but also to double their investments in schools, in housing, in protective services, in transportation, in clothing and food, and in most other areas. The capital investment required will equal the total of all savings acquired by the countries of the world during recorded history.

The picture in this country parallels world trends. By 1975, the estimated population of the United States will be 225 million. In the last decade, U. S. population increased by 23 million persons, and in the next ten years 26 million new young workers will be added to the labor force. By 1970, one out of three persons in this country will be 25 years of age or younger. Enrollments at all educational levels will continue to spiral: so will investments in buildings, in teaching and administrative personnel, in equipment, services, and instructional materials.

The rapid growth of population is being paralleled by a sustained rush to great centers of population. Urbanization is reaching dramatic proportions as vast regional cities dot the American landscape. Unusual social and educational problems await solution in the "gray" areas of great urban centers.

The growth of automation and technology raise basic questions about the adequacy of current educational goals. The deployment of the working population in America is undergoing radical changes; already white-collar workers outnumber blue-collar workers, and producers of services outnumber producers of goods. Mechanization and automation are creating great expansions in professional and technical occupations and widespread technological unemployment among the untrained and uneducated. As the nation presses forward to the abundance of the semi-automatic factory, great numbers of individuals who are part of a complex process over which they have little, if any, personal control will continue to be dislocated. The importance of careful planning and clear educational goals during a period of rapid transition have been highlighted by Michael:[2]

> The long-range stability of the social system depends on a population of young people properly educated to enter the adult world of tasks and attitudes. Once, the pace of change was slow enough to permit a comfortable margin of compatibility between the adult world and the one children were trained to expect. This compatibility no longer exists. Now we have to ask: What should be the education of a population more and more enveloped in cybernation? What are the appropriate attitudes toward and training for participation in government, the use of leisure, standards of consumption, particular occupations?

Although it is difficult to judge the extent of compatibility or incompatibility in our educational, attitudinal, and occupational systems, it is clear that technology and cybernation are building powerful trends toward specialization and unprecedented demands for highly trained personnel. The shortage of such personnel is exemplified by the fact that although Los Angeles had 170,000 unemployed in 1961, firms in that city ran advertisements for skilled workers as far away as New York. It appears certain that the next 20 years will see an employment age where the professional, the highly trained technician, and the skilled craftsman will be of unparalleled importance.

Predictions indicate that the blue-collar workers will not be alone in feeling the impact of cybernation. Advances in information technology will cause major shifts in existing patterns of middle management. Predictions state that: (1) much of the present work of middle managers will be programmed, and middle management planning will increasingly become the function of operation researchers and organizational analysts, (2) recentralization will occur in large organizations, and top managers will assume even greater responsibility for initiation and planning, (3) many middle management positions will be downgraded in status while a smaller number will be lifted to the top-management level, (4) top and middle management functions will be sharply delineated, and psychological separation

---

[2] Donald N. Michael, *Cybernation: The Silent Conquest* (Santa Barbara, California: Center for the Study of Democratic Institutions, 1962), p. 41.

between the two levels will be pronounced, and (5) normal lines of advancement will be drastically curtailed.[3]

Dramatic increments of new knowledge and the impact of science are radically affecting established patterns of living. It is predicted that by the close of this century scientists will have unlocked the secret of life. They will not only be able to transform inanimate chemicals into living matter, but they will also have mastered the mysteries of cancer, viruses, and mental illness. Already dozens of Americans are dependent upon electronic devices (provided by bioelectronics) to stimulate regular functioning of weak and damaged hearts. Within a few years, electronic computers will be widely used in researching heart diseases, in checking income tax returns, in government and business decision-making, and in helping to control activities in such industries as oil, steel, and chemicals.

Moreover, science is already turning attention to practical applications of the conquest of space; to mining minerals in asteroids, to establishing instantaneous world-wide communication systems, to interplanetary communication with laser beams, and to exploration of planets in the solar system. Equally dramatic are predictions concerning the use of computers to determine future fashions; the mass production of unique materials for industrial and home construction; the designing of automobiles that ride on cushions of air; the pre-packaging of commuters for swift transportation by monorail; and the miniaturizing of mass-communications equipment.

The growth of knowledge is vividly illustrated by the fact that an estimated 40,000 books and articles are being issued weekly by the presses of the world. Established school curricula are melting before the advance of new knowledge in most fields. The rapid obsolescence of knowledge in modern times is prompting basic questions concerning the foci of curricula adequate for the preparation of future citizens. What knowledge is of most worth for effective functioning in tomorrow's world? How can learners and teachers keep abreast of new knowledge? How may adults with obsolete knowledges and skills be retrained and

---

[3] See Harold J. Leavitt and Thomas L. Whisler, "Management in the 1980's," *Harvard Business Review* (Nov., Dec., 1958), pp. 41-48.

re-educated? Such questions will acquire increased significance with the continuing development of science and new knowledge.

Rapid shifts are occurring in world conceptions of morals, power, economics, and freedom. Will Durant has pointed out in *The Story of Civilization* that a new moral code based on urbanism rather than ruralism is being forged in our time. To Durant, "the changes of belief . . . are more important than the changes in the balance of power. At the present time there are millions of people in Western Europe and America who no longer believe in the old diety. Probably half the people in Russia no longer believe." Other historians are pointing toward new levels of economic and social standing for the average citizen; toward increased racial equality for minorities; toward accelerated change in newly-developing countries; and toward an uneasy world climate where international power problems will necessitate living with crises, dilemmas, and insoluble problems.

The forces surrounding the schools are powerful and pervasive; they are creating strong societal demands that quantity in education be matched with quality and that universality be paralleled by excellence. Underlying these forces are fundamental questions which relate to the purpose and meaning of large educational organizations in modern society. The pressure of change is causing us to look beyond the frontiers of science, to questions of ultimate value. The essential questions relate to the continued maintenance and growth of democracy in the wider world. How may democracy survive and flourish in a world where there are forceful and determined conflicting ideologies? How may automation and technology be used constructively without major disruptions in society? How may the development of science, with its major financial demands both within government and the larger society, be wisely and intelligently controlled? What is the meaning of great shifts in moral codes and value patterns? All of these questions have important implications for schools in modern society.

Swift social change has highlighted the critical need for sound appraisal and analysis of the appropriate professional and social roles of educational leaders. Of the factors affecting excellence

5

in school systems, probably none is more important than the educational leaders who have responsibility for recommending changes in educational policy, for selecting teachers, for determining curriculum, and for facilitating learning. Not only are these leaders in strategic positions to shape the directions in which educational institutions move, but also they can play significant roles in affecting the performance level of these institutions. Accordingly, plans to recruit effective school leaders, to define clearly their professional and social roles, and to conceptualize appropriate pre-service and in-service programs for their preparation are essential if educational institutions are to meet the challenges of change. Progress along these fronts is important for several reasons.

First, the importance of education is being determined and judged on a much larger stage than ever before. No longer are contributions of educational leaders judged to be of importance only within the contexts of local school districts; education has attained national and international significance. Today, the educational administrator is the key leader of a significant social institution. Effectiveness in his position requires breadth and vision in comprehending the meaning of widespread change, and wisdom in assessing the implications of change for the educational enterprise. Equally important, the educational leader requires the stature and competence necessary for formulating and promoting educational policy in a highly complex matrix of social and ideological conflict.

Second, technology, cybernation, the growth of science and new knowledge, and the redeployment of America's working force carry implications for the kind of education necessary for effective living in the society of the future. Educational planning to meet these challenges will require movement in several directions. Initially, it will be necessary to make careful assessments of occupational and social needs 10 to 20 years into the future. Such assessments will be required as a base for planning the social, intellectual, and attitudinal preparation of present learners. Periodic adjustments will be necessary to meet unanticipated changes in the advance of technology and cybernation. New learning experiences and guidance activities will need to be developed (a) to cope with the drop-out problem, (b) to direct learners into fields where technological unemployment is least likely, and (c) to equip learners with attitudes that will assist them in grappling with their citizenship responsibilities in the modern world.

There can be little doubt that tomorrow's educational leader will need to assume an increasingly important social role in promoting constructive solutions to major societal problems through education. Upon these leaders will fall significant responsibilities for forging societal and professional agreements concerning the directions of education in the public schools. The rate of change in American society is exponential rather than linear; sound leadership in continuously reappraising educational directions will become increasingly mandatory in the years ahead.

Third, rapid shifts in world conceptions of morals, power, economics, and freedom highlight the importance of school leadership in the resolution of major educational dilemmas facing our society. The past decade has witnessed an increased and broadened interest in education from all segments of our society; much of this interest has been generated by conflicting values in relation to important educational issues. Social controversy will continue to characterize our society in relation to significant value-laden issues such as integration, the provision of equal educational opportunity, the basis of adequate financial support, and local versus federal control. Thus, educational leaders will function in a milieu of increasing complexity where social forces will generate incompatible educational expectations and problems of unusual societal import. Equipping school administrators to provide professional leadership in the resolution of community value dilemmas is a high priority challenge in our time.

Significant tasks face those who have responsibility for structuring pre-service and in-service preparation programs for school leaders. Of primary importance in our time is the task of image definition—of conceptualizing the appropriate professional and social roles of leaders who will function in significant social institutions. The projection of new forms of leadership excellence will require inventiveness based upon new insights, new approaches, and new perspectives; account will need to be taken

7

of pervasive national and international influences affecting education, of population growth and mobility, of metropolitanism, of technology and cybernation, of advances in science and the growth of knowledge, of societal demands for educational excellence, and of shifting national and world values. The educational leader of the future will function in an increasingly complex environment; the stature of his image should equal the challenges he will be required to encompass.

Chapter II

Perspectives of Public Administration

JOHN D. MILLETT
President,
Miami University

The study of public administration in the United States has suffered from two grievous defects: a confusion of objective and a confusion of content. Some understanding of the various factors involved in these confusions may well provide assistance in the development and improvement of efforts to educate administrators, whether they be public school officials or others.

From the beginning of systematic study of governmental administrative activity, in the 1880's, there has been uncertainty whether public administration should seek primarily to advance our knowledge about government, or should seek a more practical purpose of improving the conduct of administrative operations. This uncertainty has by no means been confined to the study of public administration. It may indeed be part of a larger story of the very history of all education in the United States.

After the Civil War there was in large measure a revolt against the classical curriculum in higher education which had dominated the eighteenth century and the early nineteenth century college. Higher education, it was widely said, should be practical. Actually, higher education in colonial and then independent America had always envisaged practical purposes. The difficulty was that the classical curriculum no longer met the needs of a nation rapidly growing in industrial endeavor. The various fields of learning, stimulated by German example, were seeking new knowledge and a broader utility than had ever been conceived possible in ante-bellum days.

We cannot stop here to indulge in intellectual history. It is sufficient to observe only that a lively interest in practical affairs as well as the accumulation of extensive factual data were characteristic of the new "science" to be discovered in social as well as in physical and biological phenomena. Moreover, the philosophers of the new era were asserting that truth was to be found in the consequences of ideas.

In a very real sense the confusion of objective in the study of public administration arose from a failure to observe a now well understood distinction: the distinction between science and technology, the distinction between knowledge and the application of knowledge to everyday problems, the distinction between a discipline and a professional field. While this distinction is, as I have said, well understood today, it is a distinction which continues to be bothersome in observance. The fact appears to be that in any area in which we endeavor to apply human reason to human behavior and environment we find a close relationship between knowledge as science and knowledge as the art of action.

The disciplines as scientific knowledge are concerned with the formulation of theories, generalizations, or "laws" which provide us with concepts integrating the world of fact and providing predictable elements of future behavior. The professions as the art of knowledge cannot wait for science to formulate its concepts and test them for conformance with fact. The professions hand us the best available data from human experience and wisdom to guide us in solving immediate and perplexing issues, from a concern for health and justice to the launching of missiles and the administration of a school system.

We now realize that science and art in any field of human interest must interact, must each contribute to both the expansion of knowledge and the improvement of individual well-being. Action based upon empirical data may be wasteful, even a failure. Experience to be meaningful and continually valuable must be analyzed and synthesized into conceptual schemes which advance our understanding or encourage still further experimentation and formulation of concepts.

A failure clearly to comprehend the difference between those elements of the study of public administration concerned with the advancement of knowledge and those concerned with the solution of practical problems has plagued scholars for many years. This failure has been evident, too, in the content of such studies. Prescription of desirable practice has run ahead of concepts of governmental institutions and process. Indeed, many suggestions for action have not been carefully formulated in terms of empirical evidence. The result is that the study of public administration today is seeking to clarify concepts and to broaden its factual base while still advancing the cause of administrative improvement.

There are two other introductory comments which are relevant to the purpose of this paper. I shall concentrate attention upon public administration as part of the discipline of political science and upon administration as a part of the institutional structure and political process of government. In practice, other disciplines such as sociology, economics, and social psychology may contribute substantially to our knowledge of the administrative process. Our point of view here is primarily political.

It must also be mentioned that political scientists are necessarily influenced in their study by the major political issues of the time and place in which they labor. To ignore current problems is to remove any study from association with those stubborn facts and tests of experience upon which our knowledge is so largely built. Yet concentration upon the immediately relevant is apt to leave great gaps in the accumulation of systematic knowledge. Thus, the study of public administration early gave attention to problems of municipal government when this was the major governmental concern of our society. More recently, many studies have concentrated upon federal administration because this activity became so pervasive and vital in American social and political survival. Today, international and comparative study occupy much time and interest. Yet problems of state and local governmental administration are much with us, even if less glamorous in terms of current excitement. The study of public administration has too often forgotten to test its concepts and observations in this arena of government.

I am scarcely prepared to suggest how an analytical survey of the study of public administration may provide "new" perspectives for the education of school administrators. At best I

11

can but hope that "old" perspectives drawn from the study of public administration may afford some insights, and some warnings, for those now seeking to advance further the professional competence of public school officials.

POLITICS AND ADMINISTRATION

An early scholar in the field of public administration, Professor Frank J. Goodnow of Columbia University, later president of the Johns Hopkins University, argued that the governmental process consisted of two basic parts: politics and administration.[1] The work of legislative, executive, and judicial branches constituted the politics of government. Professor Goodnow did not look beyond these formal organs of decision-making to the political structure of society, including political parties and pressure groups. The other fundamental element of government was administration, the actual performance of governmental activities authorized by the political element.

This distinction between politics and administration has been much criticized by political scientists.[2] It seemed to suggest that administrative officials should faithfully carry out those policies given to them by the political process and otherwise should separate themselves from any concern with the formulation and enactment of policy. In fact, we know that administrators can and do have an active role in developing and advocating public policy, which is the very heart of political activity. Administrators are often professionals in a technical field of governmental endeavor. They must give legislators, executive, and judiciary the benefit of expert advice. Governmental policy cannot be formulated in a political vacuum, apart from concern for administrative experience and administrative know-how.

At the same time the distinction proposed by Professor Goodnow as a basic concept of our governmental institutions is a very important one. Indeed, it seems probable that its importance has never been sufficiently appreciated or adequately

---

[1] Frank J. Goodnow, *Politics and Administration* (New York: the Macmillan Company, 1900).

[2] For example, see Paul H. Appleby, *Policy and Administration* (University, Alabama: University of Alabama Press, 1949).

discussed by political scientists. The distinction, for example, is fundamental to the development of a merit or career system of administrative recruitment. The distinction is vital to professionalization of the public service. No one attached to democratic ideals would suggest that political decisions must be dominated by a permanent bureaucracy or a professional elite in society. In our governmental practice there must be some difference between political action and administrative action.

If there is no workable distinction between politics and administration, then the only avenue to a responsible bureaucracy is an impermanent system of administrative recruitment. Each change in the political party or factional control of government, to be effective in policy-making, must bring with it all new administrative personnel. The price of administrative domination of public policy is administrative expendability. The price of administrative professionalization is loyalty to the political leadership in control of government.

Our administrative activity today is too highly technical to propose that any citizen may be competent to perform it. Our military defense, our scientific research, our public health, our foreign affairs, our educational endeavor—every one and many more besides require expert staffing. Administrative efficiency demands administrative professionalization. But our democratic political system requires that government be responsive to the elected representatives of the people. A democratic polity demands responsible administrative behavior.

This was the central issue which Professor Goodnow was attempting to present at the very beginning of this century. It is an issue which still deserves the most serious discussion in any and every field of governmental endeavor.

Only incidentally and somewhat tangentially have scholars of public administration considered the problem of relationship in political decision-making between elected and appointed representatives of the people on the one hand and professional administrators on the other hand. When the budget reform movement was getting under way in this country, one critic argued that to give the chief executive authority to collect and review the appropriation estimates of administrative agencies

13

would result in a substantial increase in executive power vis-a-vis legislative power.[3] The response of budget enthusiasts was that the authority of the executive to review appropriation requests of administrative agencies was intended only to improve the mechanism of executive supervision. The executive budget, it was pointed out, would in nowise alter the power of the legislature to make an independent judgment about administrative needs.[4]

During the 1920's a leading political scientist decided that it was necessary to develop some theory of administrative supervision for the American system of government. He propounded the startling doctrine that the legislature was all-powerful in the direction and control of administrative activity.[5] For reasons of convenience and feasibility, however, Professor Willoughby argued that the legislature should delegate its power of administrative supervision to the executive. In the federal government the President was to be regarded as the agent of the Congress in watching over administration. What such a concept of legislative-executive relationships implied for the American structure of legislative, executive, and judicial independence, Professor Willoughby did not say.

In 1937 the President's Committee on Administrative Management, in presenting far-reaching proposals for executive management in the federal government, realized that it would have in some way to justify its recommendations in political and constitutional terms. The Committee was composed of a political scientist distinguished in the field of political theory, a political scientist distinguished in the study of public administration, and a professional administrator. The Committee argued persuasively that a democratic system of government amid the perplexities of the twentieth century must have effective leadership. Only the executive under our system of government could exercise such leadership. It was therefore necessary, indeed urgent, the

[3] Edward A. Fitzgerald, *Budget Making in a Democracy* (New York: the Macmillan Company, 1918).

[4] Frederick A. Cleveland and Arthur E. Buck, *The Budget and Responsible Government* (New York: the Macmillan Company, 1920).

[5] W. F. Willoughby, *Principles of Public Administration* (Baltimore: the Johns Hopkins Press, 1927).

14

Committee insisted, to provide the executive with management tools which would enable him effectively to supervise the administrative activities of government.[6] It was apparently assumed that the executive must direct the formulation and administration of public policy in order for dynamic governmental leadership to realize its objectives.

In general, the President's Committee on Administrative Management avoided any discussion of executive-legislative relationships in our system of government. That such relationships might be more crucial than administrative supervision in achieving the goals of dynamic leadership was largely ignored. In only one field of executive management did the Committee acknowledge legislative interest in administrative affairs. This was the field of governmental accounting, where an agency of the legislature, the General Accounting Office, exercised wide authority. The President's Committee wanted the authority to prescribe administrative accounting systems and to control administrative expenditures transferred from the General Accounting Office to an agency of the President. To make this proposal more palatable to legislative sensibilities, the Committee propounded the amazing doctrine of "the full accountability of the Executive to the Congress" in the field of public accounting and expenditure control. How such a system would have operated in practice, and how it would have affected the constitutional system of the United States, the President's Committee failed to explain.

Since the end of World War II a few political scientists have returned to the question of the constitutional status of public administration. The issue is a major one in understanding the governmental process in America. Constitutional doctrine in our country prescribes that the legislative, the executive, and the judicial power shall be distinct and separate one from the other. There is some commingling of power and some degree of interdependence in order to realize that consensus indispensable to any system of government. At the same time the three branches or powers are not dependent or subservient one to the other. Indeed, the founding fathers insisted that a separation of power

---

[6] President's Committee on Administrative Management, *Report With Special Studies* (Washington, D. C.: Government Printing Office, 1937).

15

was essential to the preservation of freedom. Anyone who advocates the supremacy of one power over the other two is seeking to alter the system of American government.

Difficulty arises when the political scientist confronts the emergence of the administrative state. American constitutionalism recognizes only three branches or divisions of governmental power: legislative, executive, and judicial. Where in any such tripartite scheme do the great administrative aggregations of today fit? Some—including even legislators, constitutional lawyers, and judges—have argued that administrative agencies are an extension of executive power. It has even been suggested that, if administrative agencies aren't a part of the executive branch, they ought to be.[7]

There is, however, a contrary concept held by some political scientists.[8] I have myself argued at some length that public administration—apart from that which represents in reality an institutionalizing of legislative, executive, and judicial power— should be regarded as a separate echelon of government subordinate to the direction and control of all three branches of governmental power.[9] Each power—legislative, executive, and judicial— has its separate and unique part to play in the supervision of administrative activities. Each power deals directly with agencies of administration. The power of legislative supervision is not exercised through the executive, and should not be if a separate legislative power is to be preserved. The power of executive supervision is not exercised through the legislature, and should not be if a separate executive power is to be preserved. The power of judicial supervision is not exercised through either the legislature or the executive, and should not be if a separate judicial power is to be preserved.

The American system of government does in practice recognize a distinction between politics and administration. Such a distinction is essential to a democratic polity and a constitutional

<hr>

[7] Arthur Maass, *Muddy Waters: the Army Engineers and the Nation's Rivers* (Cambridge: Harvard University Press, 1951).

[8] See Charles S. Hyneman, *Bureaucracy in a Democracy* (New York: Harper and Brothers, 1950).

[9] John D. Millett, *Government and Public Administration* (New York: McGraw-Hill Book Company, 1959).

16

system of separation of power. Here is a first and all important concept of American political science.

The Institutional Environment of Public Administration

Some further elaboration of the discussion just outlined is warranted, especially in terms of its applicability to educational administration in the United States.

There has been some disposition in recent years to suggest that the administrative process is a basic way of life in a highly specialized society.[10] Regardless of the substantive field of activity—business enterprise, hospital care, education, military protection, scientific research and development, or public administration—the administrative process is fundamentally the same.

Personally, I cannot accept this proposition. There are undoubtedly certain similarities in the management of the organized activities of society. But even in various fields of governmental endeavor there are substantive problems of values and of policy which are peculiar to the activity itself. The vital issues of foreign policy are not similar to the vital issues of education. The vital issues of military policy are not similar to the vital issues of guarding or preserving free competitive enterprise. The vital issues of public and mental health are not similar to the vital issues of conservation of natural resources. No consideration of management similarities in these varied endeavors should be permitted to obscure the far-reaching peculiar problems of each.

On a broader scale, there are fundamental differences in the institutional environment of business administration and public administration. First, business administration usually operates under conditions of the market place and receives its allocation of resources through competitive pricing. Public administration operates under the principles of public planning, and receives its allocation of resources through the political process. Secondly, business administration is subject to the test of survival and

---

[10] This position is put forth, for example, by Edward H. Litchfield, "Notes on a Theory of Administration," *Administrative Science Quarterly*, vol. 1 (June, 1956), p. 3.

growth based upon profits. Public administration is subject to the test of survival and growth based upon the performance of services as evaluated by the decision-making organs of government. Thirdly, business administration operates under a system of private responsibility for its actions, subject to general standards of conduct prescribed by government in the name of the public interest. Public administration operates under a system of public responsibility for its actions, exercised by the political instrumentalities of society. These are great differences in institutional environment, and the administrative process must necessarily reflect such differences.

No school administrator needs to be told that public education has its unique environmental characteristics. Unfortunately, few if any political scientists have examined these differences with the care they merit. For example, school administration is peculiarly local in its organizational status. Basic policies of school operation are determined in considerable degree by state law. Indeed, public education is legally considered a state government function subject to local administration. Yet it is the local school district which is the fundamental unit of operation for public education, and the district possesses governmental authority as well.

The prevailing pattern of government and administration in public education is the locally elected school board and the board appointed professional administrator. The board in effect exercises both executive and legislative power. The school superintendent is a career administrator who advises the board about educational policy, operation, and financing. He is responsible for the administration of state school law and local policy decisions.

Here is in practice a recognition of a distinction between politics and administration. The professional administrator is an expert adviser to and supervisor for a lay board which represents the community concern with public education.

Some political scientists have been critical of school organization on the ground that the local board combines legislative and executive power. They have suggested that the professional school administrator should be named by a local government executive—the mayor of a city presumably—and the appropriation-taxation authority should be exercised by the local legislature.[11] It has been argued that the public interest in education can better be expressed by a locally elected executive and locally elected legislature than by a separately and locally elected board. It is also claimed that only through executive supervision can school administration be properly integrated with local planning and local finances.

Scholars in public school administration have argued that the local school board, especially one elected at special times and by nonpartisan ballot, better represents the community interest in education than a mayor and council who may be concerned with a variety of local problems. It is further argued that local consensus on the location of facilities and on school financing can be realized through avenues of informal collaboration between school and city government rather than only through executive supervision.

In particular, public education is regarded as a peculiar function of government not to be equated with any other local governmental service such as police and fire protection, water supply, street maintenance and cleaning, and public health. Personally, I subscribe to this proposition.

A different element has been introduced into school administration by the emergence of state power in the field of education. Should the federal government become even more active than at present in the field of public education, still a further complication in school organization and administration will occur.

School advocates have tended to favor administrative organization at the state level similar to that with which they have been familiar at the local level. Yet there are three vital differences between local school administration at the state and at the local level. First of all, the state school board, where such has been established, has no legislative power. School law is enacted by the state legislature, with such leadership and concurrence as the state executive may exercise. Secondly, the state school board has no appropriation or taxing power. This is also exer-

---

[11] See, for example, N. B. Henry and J. B. Kerwin, *Schools and City Government* (Chicago: University of Chicago Press, 1938).

19

cised by the legislature and executive acting concurrently. Thirdly, the state school board does not operate a school system; it supervises the operation of local school districts. Administrative supervision requires a different kind of ability and a different kind of procedure from that of administrative operation.

Here are environmental differences which appear not to have received the attention both of political scientists and of scholars of school administration which they need. Here is an important part surely of the unfinished business of the discipline of political science and of the professional field of school administration.

The Problem of Leadership

The theory of a distinction between politics and administration contains a fundamental assumption. It is that leadership in the advocacy and adoption of important policies and objectives will be provided by the political element of government. The task of administration is to advise this political element, and to implement the decisions determined through the political process.

As political scientists have studied leadership in the American political system, they have tended to concentrate their attention upon the federal level of government. In consequence, they have been concerned especially to analyze presidential leadership.[12] Administrative assistance has been provided to strengthen and institutionalize executive leadership. At the state level much of the same kind of development has taken place, although in a less elaborate way and with much less attention.[13] At the local level of government the issue of leadership has also tended to receive little attention, although there has been some debate

---

[12] Among the many studies on presidential leadership, see particularly Pendleton Herring, *Presidential Leadership* (New York: Farrar and Rinehart, Inc., 1940); Wilfred E. Binkley, *President and Congress* (New York: Alfred A. Knopf, 1947); Louis Brownlow, *The President and the Presidency* (Chicago: Public Administration Service, 1949); Sidney Hyman, *The American President* (New York: Harper and Brothers, 1954); Clinton Rossiter, *The American Presidency* (New York: Harcourt, Brace and Company, Inc., 1956); and Richard E. Neustadt, *Presidential Power* (New York: John Wiley and Sons, Inc., 1960).

[13] The only major study at the state level has been Coleman B. Ransome, Jr., *The Office of Governor in the United States* (University, Alabama: University of Alabama Press, 1956).

whether the council-manager form of government or the strong mayor form is preferable in terms of political leadership and effective direction of administrative activity.[14]

The local school district presents a somewhat different institutional framework of leadership from that to be found in federal, state, and even local government. If any comparison is possible, it would seem most profitable to examine the council-manager arrangement for local government. In the local school district, political leadership is presumably exercised by a lay, part-time board of citizens. Administrative leadership is exercised by the professional school superintendent.

Public affairs, including educational affairs, require alert, determined, timely, intelligent, moral, and politically responsible leadership. In our system of government this type of leadership is expected to emerge as an amalgam of effort by both political officials and professional administrators. Unfortunately, it may happen under various circumstances that political officials serve on a part-time basis, or for limited periods of time. It may happen that political officials lack any general background sufficient to evaluate the policy proposals of administrative professionals, and have little or nothing to contribute to their consideration. Sometimes political leadership is reluctant to make decisions. On occasion, a community may be so evenly balanced among various interests and so lacking in public spirited citizen groups that political leadership is impossible or ineffective.

Under circumstances where political leadership is inept or even absent, the professional administrator is strongly tempted to fill the vacuum, especially when such administrative leadership has positive goals to achieve. When professional or administrative leadership assumes the task of political leadership it runs a dual risk. The administrator must cultivate sources of political support ·in the community, and must seek to manipulate the existing political leadership. This may arouse antagonisms. Furthermore,

---

[14] The only comprehensive study of the council-manager form of government remains Harold A. Stone, Don K. Price, and Kathryn H. Stone, *City Manager Government in the United States* (Chicago: Public Administration Service, 1940). On the role of the mayor in our largest, but by no means typical, city, see Wallace S. Sayre and Herbert Kaufman, *Governing New York City* (New York: Russell Sage Foundation, 1960).

the professional administrator must appear as a public advocate, which involves criticism as well as approval. The extent of one or the other can only be revealed through the electoral process. When and if he runs for public office, the professional has ceased to be an administrator and has become a political leader.

The administrator depends for his effectiveness upon political leadership, or at least political protection. In our system of government, the administrator cannot provide such leadership for himself. This is an important condition of professionalization in the public service. Ordinarily, when the administrator and political leadership are in disagreement about policies, it is the administrator who must give way. If the policy issues are of major concern to the administrator, involving his professional judgment and his personal integrity, the administrator will resign rather than continue to hold office. Fortunately, such an impasse does not often occur in our governmental system.

Political leadership remains an indispensable condition of progressive government and administration.

Organization

Early in the study of public administration, political scientists set for themselves some very practical goals. Their avowed purpose was to increase or advance efficiency and economy in government administration. This goal was never defined with any precision; its importance was taken as self-evident. Scholars of public administration were practically minded. They worked at first with city governments. Later, they concentrated attention upon the federal government and to some extent upon state governments. President Taft's Commission on Economy and Efficiency between 1910 and 1912 set the example.

Three particular subjects were commonly analyzed by the scholars of public administration in their pursuit of economy and efficiency. These were personnel administration, budget administration, and administrative organization. Such reforms were advocated as the extension of the merit system and the introduction of personnel training, the adoption of the executive budget and careful review of operating expenditures, and the integration and coordination of related agencies. These were the standards of administrative improvement.

It is unnecessary here to review the history of the administrative reform movement. We may use the subject of organizational change to illustrate the difficulties which were encountered.

First of all, it should be noted that the political scientists who became so much concerned with administrative organization gave little attention to the historical development of governmental agencies, or to the political forces which led to their creation. That the political aspects of organization should have been given so little attention seems surprising. One general study of federal government administrative history was undertaken at the end of World War I.[15] Subsequently the late Professor Leonard D. White of Chicago wrote four notable volumes tracing the history of federal government administration in terms of political issues.[16] Here the close relationship between organizational arrangements and public issues was clearly demonstrated.

The customary position on organization matters was well expressed by the President's Committee on Administrative Management in 1937. The Committee asserted: "The primary purpose of a rational reorganization of the administrative agencies of the Executive Branch of the Government is to reduce to a manageable compass the number of agencies reporting to the President."[17] Its specification of organizational faults included a multiplicity of agencies, use of boards instead of single administrators to head agencies, a chaotic field structure, and the isolation of agencies from effective presidential supervision of policy. It should be noted that the Committee made two assumptions to which we have already referred: that all administrative agencies are a part of the executive branch, and that policy supervision is only effective when provided through executive channels.

As a part of the work of the President's Committee, one of

---

[15] Lloyd M. Short, *The Development of National Administrative Organization in the United States* (Baltimore: the Johns Hopkins Press, 1923).
[16] Leonard D. White, *The Federalists* (New York: the Macmillan Company, 1948); *The Jeffersonians* (1951); *The Jacksonians* (1954); and *The Republican Era* (1958).
[17] *Report, op. cit.,* p. 31.

its members, Luther Gulick, prepared and published a paper on the technical aspects of organization.[18] This paper remains today the major presentation of governmental administrative organization as a structural system. Gulick set forth a theory of division of work, of coordination of work, and of a pattern of organization. He observed four kinds of work division: by major purpose or function, process, clientele, and place. Gulick suggested but did not elaborate a distinction between operating organization and management organization. The importance of administrative leadership was acknowledged but was discussed primarily in terms of the force of a dominant idea, such as "to win the war." In his conclusion Gulick acknowledged that from the "standpoint of organization" insufficient attention had been given to "political life and leadership."

Gulick's paper came under immediate criticism from political scientists. Professor Schuyler C. Wallace of Columbia raised some profound and far-reaching questions about the departmental structure of federal administrative agencies.[19] To what extent did the generalizations of administrative science offer an exact prescription for organizational structure? How far did differences in the nature and objective of various administrative activities warrant differences in organizational arrangements? To what extent and how should the values of liberty of the person and of property affect organizational structure? To what extent should organizational structure be expected to reflect the conflict of interest groups in society? How should organizational structure reflect the geographical diversity of the United States? Professor Wallace declared he could find no empirical evidence or acceptable theory available to answer these and other questions which he posed.

The task of criticism was carried still further by Professor Herbert A. Simon, later of the Carnegie Institute of Technology, and by Professor Dwight Waldo of California. Simon argued that organization was essentially a problem in social psychology and

---

[18] Luther Gulick, "Notes on the Theory of Organization," in Luther Gulick and L. Urwick, eds., *Papers on the Science of Administration* (New York: Institute of Public Administration, 1937), p. 1.

[19] Schuyler C. Wallace, *Federal Departmentalization: A Critique of Theories of Organization* (New York: Columbia University Press, 1941).

could be analyzed effectively only in terms of human behavior.[20] After sketching the historical development of writings in public administration, Waldo found fault with their underlying philosophical assumptions.[21] He declared that "the Heavenly City of Twentieth Century Public Administrators" was not clearly defined in terms of the ends of the state, in terms of governmental-economic relationships, or in terms of ultimate values. The criteria of desirable action were utilitarian and pragmatic. Administrative theory, such as it was, appeared to presuppose an administrative class in society, and appeared to be deficient in handling questions of political responsibility.

These various criticisms of a structural theory of administrative organization as it had evolved from 1900 to 1940 were quite trenchant. They appear to have been so convincing that no systematic effort by a political scientist has been made since Gulick to develop a comprehensive structural theory of administrative organization.

This situation seems unfortunate, since I am by no means convinced that a structural theory is either impossible or unimportant. On the contrary, such a theory is as much needed today as it was twenty-five years ago when Gulick presented his paper. More than this, I believe the outlines of such a theory are now much clearer than ever before.

First, a structural theory must relate the purpose of administrative activity to the traditions and institutions of government in American society. Secondly, structural theory must recognize a system of political responsibility in government. In the third place, structural theory must acknowledge a power structure in the United States, and relate organization to class structure and interest groups. In the fourth place, organization structure in government must differentiate beween arrangements for institutionalizing the legislative, executive, and judicial branches of government and arrangements to carry out the operating activities

[20] Herbert A. Simon, *Administrative Behavior:* A Study of Administrative Processes in Administrative Organization (New York: the Macmillan Company, 1947).

[21] Dwight Waldo, *The Administrative State:* A Study of the Political Theory of American Public Administration (New York: the Ronald Press Company, 1948).

of government. Finally, with this context of traditions, power system, and political institutions as related to administrative purpose, there is an area of technical concern with operating organization involving division of work specializations and of geographical areas, integration and coordination of work processes, and effective leadership.[22]

In the past 15 years most discussions of organization have been devoted to the development of a behavioral theory. It is not clear that these efforts have in fact developed a consistent and systematic set of generalizations or principles about organization. There is no doubt that these discussions have advanced our understanding of organization.[23]

In general, an organization brings together at least four different types of persons. First, there are the operators, the front-line workers who man a production plant, sell the products, or provide a service to the public. Secondly, there are the supervisors on the job who direct and check the work done by the operators. Thirdly, many organizations require a variety of specialists who plan the technical aspects of the job and provide various services which make possible the basic work of an organization. Finally, there are the managers who bring workers, supervisors, and specialists into a necessary harmonious whole.

In the organized relationships which exist among these various types of persons, three basic situations occur. First, every person regardless of his level of ability and job assignment experiences certain felt needs: a sense of usefulness, recognition of effort, and consideration as an individual. Secondly, formal relationships based upon an assignment of authority will be supplemented by informal relationships based upon group response to a natural leader or group sense of common interest. Thirdly, there is often real or latent conflict between those in authority and others.

---

[22] See Edwin O. Stene, *Some Thoughts on the Theory and Practice of Public Administration,* Indiana Business Information Bulletin No. 38 (Bloomington: Indiana University School of Business, 1960).

[23] The generalizations and interpretations which follow are my own. From a wide variety of writings on behavioral theory I wish to acknowledge my particular indebtedness to James G. March and Herbert A. Simon, *Organizations* (New York: John Wiley and Sons, Inc., 1958); and Robert Tannenbaum, Irving R. Weschler, and Fred Massarik, *Leadership and Organization:* A Behavioral Science Approach (New York: McGraw-Hill Book Company, 1961).

One of the deep-seated traditions of our society is the dignity and worth of the individual. Hierarchical relationships of authority appear to challenge this tradition.

The recognition of these behavioral characteristics of individuals brought together in the working relationships of an organization has done much to achieve a more sophisticated kind of performance by managers and supervisors. It has not been easy, however, to build a realization of behavioral factors into a system of organizational prescription. Beyond the admonition that supervisors and managers must be considerate of other persons as individuals, and must provide a sense of participation in the enterprise and a reward of effort, we have not made too much progress toward a behavioral science of organization.

The studies and the discussion which have taken place do give us a number of maxims which illustrate or refine the generalizations just outlined. A few of these may be mentioned. A formalistic structure of authority and carefully prescribed rules of procedure tend to reduce individual initiative and promote a rigidity of action. The greater the personal satisfaction the individual finds in his work, the higher is his morale and his output. The greater the prestige of an organization, the greater the propensity of an individual to seek identification with it. Organizational equilibrium depends upon motivation, and motivation depends upon a balancing of contribution and inducement. Conflict arises in an organization when decisions are unacceptable to large numbers of individuals, because the probable outcome fails to meet standards of satisfaction or because the probable outcome is too uncertain. Conflict may be resolved by problem-solving, persuasion, bargaining, or an appeal to political support. Organization structure is goal-oriented and adaptive. Innovation is necessary when changing circumstances require the introduction of new programs or new standards of performance. Change is most readily acceptable when the criteria of individual and group satisfaction are observed, and when daily routines or programmed activities are altered gradually. The essence of effective organization is communication.

Such maxims as these will readily commend themselves to persons with extensive experience in organizational activity.

Most of them have acquired substantial validity from observed fact. These generalizations constitute an advance in organizational knowledge. They do not exhaust the subject as a field of inquiry, and they do not afford us yet with a comprehensive theory of the behavioral characteristics of organization.

PUBLIC ADMINISTRATION AS PUBLIC MANAGEMENT

The consideration of organizational issues just reviewed brought with it a new concept of public administration: the concept of management. Here the field of business administration seems to have provided the precedent. In 1937 the President's Committee on Administrative Management applied the concept of management to the work of the President of the United States, with far-reaching results in the institutionalization of the executive in the American system of government. The 1937 report was a major development in the theory and practice of public administration.

In time it came to be perceived that the principal management level of public administration is that of the department, agency, or other operating entity of governmental enterprise. The goal of management is the effective performance of government service. Within the limits of legal authorization and under such policy guidance as may be properly provided through the executive, legislative, and judicial branches of government, administrative officials of an operating enterprise seek to carry out their service under certain standards of performance. These standards involve satisfactory service (timely, adequate, equitable, and progressive), ethical service, and politically responsible service. In realizing these standards of service, management in public enterprise encounters certain common problems: problems of work direction (planning, communications, supervision, and public relations); problems of work operation (organizing, budgeting and accounting, personnel, legal procedure, and work improvement); and problems of internal service (plant construction and maintenance, purchasing, transportation, and facilities for communication).[24]

---

[24] John D. Millett, *Management in the Public Service* (New York: McGraw-Hill Book Company, 1954).

This concept of management has encountered little criticism. Perhaps it has been accepted as a common-sense description of administrative action without particular reason for comment. Perhaps it has been brushed aside as less exciting than other emerging concepts, especially that of decision-making, as the essence of the administrative process.

Public Administration as Policy Development

Because of dissatisfaction with the progress made in the analysis of organizational structure as the basis for the understanding of public administration, some political scientists have been searching for new approaches. Some thought was given to the possibility that public administration might be studied in terms of policy development. The very heart of the administrative process are the policy decisions which guide administrative action. If some meaningful generalizations could be found about policy as formulated and administered by government, then the role and functioning of administrative agencies could be clarified. At least this was the hope.

Moreover, there appeared at the outset to be two or three major advantages to this approach. For one thing, it would concentrate attention upon the substance of administration rather than upon mechanics. Too much concern had been given to procedures when the most important aspect of any administrative endeavor is the particular purpose or goal it exists to realize. For another thing, the study of policy development would avoid argument about a distinction between "politics" and "administration." The relative roles of administrators, executives, and legislators in the formulation and determination of basic policies could be examined in the context of their content. It might even be possible to develop a policy "science" which would achieve a new synthesis in the study of government, public administration, economics, and social psychology.[25]

The concept of a science of policy has not proven fruitful.

---

[25] Harold Lasswell and Daniel Lerner, eds., *The Policy Sciences:* Recent Developments in Scope and Method (Stanford: Stanford University Press, 1951); and Harold Stein, *Public Administration and Policy Development: A Case Book* (New York: Harcourt, Brace and Company, 1952).

Policy, it appears, is discrete. Policy is an inherent element of the substance of public administration, and substance varies from agency to agency. Policy arises in broad fields of government activity: foreign affairs, national security, conservation, transportation, fiscal and monetary affairs, education, welfare, health, and many other fields. The substantive issues of policy in each of these fields have little in common. Few if any persons can hope to master all the issues which require public action. The common denominators in policy questions are the process of decision-making and the process of action. The substance of policy development has defied meaningful generalization.

A Science of Decision-Making

Accordingly, from the substance of policy, scholars have turned their tools of analysis to the process of decision-making. The administrative process is described as a cycle of action consisting of decisions made by administrators.[26] Just who is to be identified as administrators has not been made clear. Moreover, the exact relationship between decision-making and action deserves some attention. The two are not necessarily always the same, as scholars of administrative behavior have been quick to point out.

Chancellor Litchfield of the University of Pittsburgh has observed that decision-making in its rational, deliberative, discretionary, and purposive form, is characterized by a definite pattern of procedure. An issue must be identified and defined, an existing situation must be analyzed, alternative courses of action to achieve a desired objective must be calculated, the desired results and desired means must be reviewed, and a definite choice of action must be determined. Decisions are a composite of values, facts, and assumptions. Each or all of these may be subject to change from time to time. Decision-making, therefore, is not a one-time activity but rather a continuing enterprise.

Secondly, Chancellor Litchfield points out that decisions involve policies (the definition of objectives), resources (people,

---

[26] Edward H. Litchfield, "Notes on a Theory of Administration," *Administrative Science Quarterly,* vol. 1 (June, 1956), p. 3.

money, materials, and authority), and means of execution (integration and synthesis). Insofar as the value content of these types of decision is concerned, he identifies three major values. Policy decisions seek purposive action. Resource decisions seek economy of operation. Execution decisions seek coordination of action.

In the third place, Chancellor Litchfield relates the decision-making process to a larger context. The dimensions of decision-making are described as a social and political environment, the nature and characteristics of the enterprise itself including its technical procedures, and the personality of the administrator. Litchfield observes that an enterprise generally seeks to perpetuate itself, to preserve its internal well-being, to maintain its status in relation to other agencies, and to realize growth in its output.

This outline for the analysis of decision-making is presented by Chancellor Litchfield as a theory of administrative process. In its outline certainly this theory provides a comprehensive model. Whether such a theory represents a substantial advance over the other approaches to the study of public administration mentioned here, no one can say with any degree of certainty. I suspect that much of what Litchfield outlines becomes comprehensible and useful only after a good deal of extensive study utilizing all available knowledge about public administration.

Professor Simon has presented decision-making from a somewhat different and a more restricted perspective.[27] He emphasizes decision-making as a procedure. He divides decisions into two types: programmed and non-programmed. Programmed decisions are those handled on a routine, repetitive basis through specific processes developed within an organization for dealing with continuing or recurring situations. Non-programmed decisions are the unique, one-time, specific actions taken to meet special situations or problems.

For both types of decisions Professor Simon postulates traditional and modern techniques of decision-making. The traditional method of handling programmed decisions is through a well-defined organizational structure with a system of sub-goals,

---

[27] Herbert A. Simon, *The New Science of Management Decision* (New York: Harper and Brothers, 1960).

31

common expectations, and standardized operating procedures, reinforced by routine long established. For the non-programmed decision the traditional technique has been the careful selection and training of managers, who utilize tradition, personal judgment, and rules of thumb in resolving important problems.

The modern techniques of making programmed decisions entail operations research and electronic data processing. To be sure, situations subject to such modern techniques must be susceptible of expression in terms of a mathematical model, with a criterion function and available empirical estimates of the numerical parameters. Any problem situation not subject to statement in terms of a mathematical model obviously cannot be analyzed with the assistance of electronic data processing. Furthermore, Professor Simon suggests that our knowledge of problem-solving may advance to the point where the very process of human thought itself can be simulated by an electronic computer. Thus would a modern technique of non-programmed decision-making be added to the arsenal of management.

This outline of decision-making procedures is useful insofar as it goes. Undoubtedly so-called modern techniques of programmed decision-making will become increasingly popular as managerial competence in quantitative analysis advances. Whether simulation of problem-solving processes will prove possible and advantageous, future experience will have to demonstrate.

Yet there appear to be definite limitations to Professor Simon's modern techniques of decision-making. Will it be possible to reduce recurring situations to mathematical models? Will it be possible to simulate social tradition and values, institutional environment, and individual judgment as the framework within which human problem-solving must operate? As a procedure, Professor Simon's outline offers a helpful guide-line to action. But this procedure can scarcely be expected to substitute for content, which remains the heart of the decision-making process.

The discussion of decision-making which is now going on provides further insight about the administrative process in our society. It seems doubtful, at least at this stage, whether a concentration upon decision-making will provide the desired synthesis of administrative knowledge. If it does, it will have to be developed, I believe, along the outlines proposed by Chancellor Litchfield.

CONCLUSION

This discussion has endeavored in historical and analytical terms to sketch the scope and content of present knowledge about public administration. In terms of the application of this knowledge to the education of administrators for our public school system, two basic questions necessarily arise. One is that of the extent to which it may be useful or even important to incorporate this knowledge into the educational program for school administrators. The second question is whether the development of knowledge in public administration may suggest new lines of endeavor in an understanding of school administration.

I do not feel competent to answer either of these questions in any detail. I assume that those who teach and those who practice school administration are familiar in a general way with the major writings in public administration, some of which have been cited herein. I assume further that both the teaching and practice of school administration are founded solidly upon an accumulated personal experience acquired specifically within the context of our public school system.

Undoubtedly, competence in school administration begins with competence in the essentials of the learning process in our society: the social goals of learning, the psychological factors in learning, the methods or procedures of learning, the subject-matter content of learning, the aids to learning such as laboratories and libraries, the physical development of youth, and the physical and mental health of youth.

The political institution of public school education conditions the administrative process. Historically, there has evolved a pattern of local school districts with lay members and professional administrators, a state school board and a state professional administrator, and a federal department with a Commissioner of Education. The relationship between these various levels of educational jurisdiction seem to be undergoing considerable change. At the same time this political institution with its tradi-

33

tions, and its structural pattern cannot be isolated from a broader environment of social, economic, and political process. Indeed, I would suggest that it is this inter-relationship of institutions and of process which constitutes in particular a new frontier of exploration for the school administrator.

The professional school administrator occupies a hazardous position, one increasingly exposed to public expectation and public criticism. In a time when knowledge about the learning process was less extensive, and when school operation was relatively simple, communication and consensus between administrators, lay board members, and parents and public may have been much simpler than today. The lay board now must rely heavily upon the professional administrator for advice and for action. Parents and public reserve the privilege of criticism while becoming farther and farther removed from an understanding of learning goals and procedures. The problem of school leadership is emerging in a new setting. I wonder if this situation has been carefully delineated and fully discussed.

Leadership in a social context and in a framework of political institutions is only a part of the challenge to school administration. The professional administrator must understand and master the process of administration itself. He must see this in terms of a structure of organization, of a system of inter-personal behavior, of a process of management, and of a procedure for decision-making. It is necessary at present to comprehend all four such points of view, since in any given situation one approach alone may be an insufficient or misleading guide to action.

The educational administrator has much knowledge which he may draw from the disciplines of political science, economics, sociology, history, and social psychology as well as from his own particular experience. Undoubtedly, these disciplines have much experience from school administration which they could profitably incorporate into their own generalizations. Perhaps more than other needs, the future presents an increasing demand for effective collaboration between scholars of various social science disciplines and school administrators, both practitioners and teachers. Such collaboration could do much to advance both the science and art of administration.

34

Chapter III

Preparing School Administrators:
Some Problems and Issues

Egbert S. Wengert
*Head of the Department
of Political Science,
Universtiy of Oregon*

This paper focuses on some limited but difficult issues in educating school administrators. They appear quickly enough as we consider a number of well-known facts. First, the scholarly study of human behavior has made great advances in recent years. Consider, for example, the impressive range of propositions that March and Simon have assembled in their recent volume *Organizations*.[1] We can also note the scope of their selected but extensive bibliography. Indeed, from each of the major disciplines in the social sciences tremendous numbers of empirical and significant theoretical studies evidently bear on the management of human affairs.

But those who work at the tasks of management, especially in our school systems, confront in the very richness of these resources the problem of abundance. Faced with the pressures of immediate decision-making, the administrator of a school cannot but be impatient with the scholar's complicated and conditional "answers" to the mounting daily problems. He may find the scholar's jargon irritating; and when the scholar investigates human behavior with the help of mathematical tools, the administrator is apt to throw up his hands in annoyance.

Yet the work of the behavioral scientists is often sufficiently impressive to command the attention of even the busiest admin-

---

[1] James G. March and Herbert A. Simon, *Organizations* (New York: John Wiley and Son, Inc., 1958).

istrator. If he has read Stuart Chase's *Proper Study of Mankind*,[2] he knows, for example, how the social scientists helped "design pilots" for the armed forces in World War II. He knows the successes (and failures!) of the pollsters. And certainly, Madison Avenue makes money out of "buying" the expertise of those who make changes in human behavior their study. So the school administrator may also stand ready to use the social scientist to help solve his practical problems.

Like the consumer of many a product of our advanced technology, however, the administrator often lacks sufficient basis for critical assessment of the "products" of social science. In his eagerness to solve what surely are almost impossible problems, he may be victimized by the sleek and shiny gadgets that aggressive entrepreneurs of social science offer for sale.

All of this points to another basic fact: scholarly study of human behavior and administration of human affairs are not intimately connected. The kind of intimacy that, for example, Mary Parker Follett or John Dewey visualized between "participants" and "observers" has not come to be. Policy-making and decisional processes are hardly viewed in real life as "hypotheses" whose test is carried out in the course of administration. What administrators systematically record and weigh the evidence of the consequences of their actions? What scholars get access to the world of affairs in order to use it as their laboratory? And if they do use it, it is on terms to which the administrator often remains a stranger.

In this context we can define the problem of educating school administrators as preparing men and women for difficult tasks by putting at their disposal the best of our resources in the social sciences. How make use of the large and enlarging resources of scholarly study of human behavior to inform and guide prospective administrators? How bridge the gap between scholars and practitioners? How establish a fruitful dialogue by means of which the scholar tests the relevance of his efforts against the tasks of administration? How enable the administrator to draw most fully on the resources of the social sciences, using them

---

[2] Stuart Chase, *The Proper Study of Mankind: An Inquiry into the Science of Human Relations* (New York: Harper and Brothers, 1948).

critically and in sophisticated awareness of their potential and limitations? Finally, how educate administrators who will become, in effect, self-conscious participant-observers who help significantly advance our understandings of administration?

To these questions there are no ready answers. Indeed, it is probably a strategic error to begin a search for answers. What may yield the most rewarding results may instead be the building of institutions and processes by which the search for answers can be initiated and carried on. These in turn may bring to light unanticipated consequences of the quest, enabling us to restate the problem with the advantage of many feedbacks from accumulating experience.

While he is describing the process in the larger terms of the society, John Dewey's observations of some 35 years ago are immediately relevant here:

> When we say that thinking and beliefs should be experimental, not absolutistic, we have in mind a certain logic of method, not, primarily, the carrying on of experimentation like that of laboratories. Such a logic involves the following factors: First, that those concepts, general principles, theories and dialectical developments which are indispensable to any systematic knowledge be shaped and tested as tools of inquiry. Secondly, that policies and proposals for social action be treated as working hypotheses, not as programs to be rigidly adhered to and executed. They will be experimental in the sense that they will be entertained subject to constant and well-equipped observation of the consequences they entail when acted upon, and subject to real and flexible revision in the light of observed consequences. . . . Differences of opinion in the sense of differences of judgment as to the course which it is best to follow, the policy which it is best to try out, will still exist. But opinion in the sense of beliefs formed and held in the absence of evidence will be reduced in quantity and importance. No longer will views generated in view of special situations be frozen into absolute standards and masquerade as eternal truths.[3]

If we change the terms of this advice to limit its scope to the processes of educating administrators we can lay some foundations for a strategy that yields some clues for inquiry, for proposals for action, for tests of them, and for the ongoing process

---

[3] John Dewey, *The Public and Its Problems* (New York: Henry Holt and Company, 1927), pp. 202-203.

of revision. But like all human enterprise, this work will not ever be finished; the answers will never be altogether clear or final.

In the university exists a framework of institutions and process by means of which we can move ahead. We might think of the professional school of education as the "broker" to evolve and test new linkages between the social scientists and the practitioners of administration. We might think of the broker as setting up the machinery for the dialogue between the two worlds, as helping to translate the communications between them, as assisting each to sharpen and improve what it gets from and gives to the other.

This brokerage is, of course, going on now. To meet the issues of educating school administrators, it may need refinement and strengthening. We might begin with inquiry into the very process of brokerage itself to know more clearly what the broker must do.

Can we, as an initial step, clarify for ourselves the role of the school administrator? In part, we confront here a theoretical and conceptual problem; in part, we need a larger range of empirical studies of administrators designed to assist in supplying the most informative "job descriptions."

Can we, as a second step, specify the nature of the demands on the administrators of our schools? For what must their education prepare them? To put it more sharply: what must the social scientists particularly bring to the education of school administrators? In what terms must the social scientists communicate in order to inform prospective school administrators?

Can we, as a third step, take fullest advantage of the characteristics of our institutions for higher education to prepare school administrators? Inquiry into institutional processes may enable us to evolve proposals for action, to test and revise them as our experience may indicate. However, that this step may be carried forward in the spirit of experimentation as Dewey suggests, our schools of education particularly need to become brokers between the universities and the profession for radical proposals, systematic assessment of educational programs, and continuous revision.

To each of these steps for the analysis of the brokerage of the school of education the following comments are directed. They are offered in the spirit of inquiry, as some starting points of further study along what may, hopefully, prove to be fruitful areas for experimental action.

CLARIFYING THE ROLE OF THE SCHOOL ADMINISTRATOR

How can we most usefully conceive of the men and women who administer our schools? We have over the years developed some popular conceptions and conventional ways of describing the job of the school administrator. We begin, for example, by noting how the state and local governments carry the major burden of public education. At the very center of educational administration we often put the local school district. We picture it as more or less autonomous, governed as a rule by a locally elected board of directors. Under general state laws and regulations, these directors typically choose an appropriate officer to carry on the day-to-day business of managing the schools. He is the superintendent. And when we talk about the "school administrator" we perhaps most generally have this official in mind.

If we were to probe this conceptualization more fully, it might be possible to discover important values it reflects. Indeed, much that is written about the school administrator shares key elements of American political ideology. The constitutional nature of the Federal system, the value of local autonomy, the rejection of "politics" as a threat to good public education, the universal competence of John Q. Public to select his school directors and even to determine large questions of policy (whether as a voter or as himself a director), the separation of the spheres of "policy" and "administration"—these are illustrative of some of the values of school administration shaped within American politics. So a powerful ideology surrounds the work of the school administrator. In part, it may confine him by demanding a commitment from him; in part, it may challenge him to review and restate his values; in part, it may help him create new bases for community action.

Another popular conception sees the school administrator at the center of a large-scale organization. Like Weber and his latter-day followers (Philip Selznick, for example), we may think of policy taking shape outside the organization. Weber regards a bureaucracy as an extremely efficient "tool" for achieving the goals of a group or a community. Selznick writes about the "organizational weapon" (the Communist Party) as used in political warfare by the master-minds of Communism. Thus, "policy" and "administration" can be kept distinct—policies are prescribed for administration to carry out. The legal model of "master-servant" states the division of responsibility between policy-maker and administrator.

We need to move beyond these classical models, however, to encompass what school administrators actually do. From descriptions of their behavior, for example, we know that they make notable contributions to the goals of public education. They seek to move their communities to identify their educational needs in terms that they, as professionals, have helped to create. In this function we can observe how the administrator, in a very important sense, seeks to modify the policies to be pursued by those who collectively make up the school "system" where he works.

The children and young people in the schools, their parents, voters, taxpayers, other officials, those who supply the goods and services required in the schools, the school directors and the teachers—all of these and others, too, make up, in this perspective, materials to be molded into new forms as may be required by these goals. Over against these various people implicated in the work of education, school administrators stand as themselves teachers, instructors, guides, "policy-makers."

As they change the world of people around them, the administrators of our schools are, of course, building an organization. They construct, in Selznick's words, an "organizational weapon" to attack ignorance. Or as Simon views it, they put together the "building blocks" of an organization. In any case, they idealize those who take part in the venture in order to make them "things" to be manipulated, used, shaped to the ends of education. In any case, they work as policy-makers, "above" the organization, the school system; "above" those who constitute the "means" of the educational enterprise.

The administrator also works "in" the organization as he stands between the forces of change on the outside and those affected by them on the inside. He mediates the changing world for students, teachers, parents, and all of the participants in the organization of our educational enterprise. He gives change meaning, of course; but chiefly he allows those who depend on him to rest easy, as it were, while he translates the intelligence he gets about the world into strategies for controlling and directing change in it.

In part, as mediator, the administrator prepares those affected to live with a world they never knew. When Lincoln died Walt Whitman mourned our "Father Abraham" who gave us a sense of sheltering power. Every day we lose our equivalents of Father Abraham as familiar landmarks lose their meaning in a rapidly changing world. We citizens may even lay aside our personal "quest for certainty" as futile and instead turn to the administrative process to mobilize growing resources to deal effectively with the world outside.

To the school administrator we can further ascribe the tasks of communicating a sense of challenge in the fact of change. In effect, the administrator invites the members of "his" organization, the school community, to join with him in the cooperative venture to change further the world outside. In addition, we can conceive him as providing some intellectual and institutional frameworks for cooperation that will make it possible for the school community to act on the world. In organizing them for "his" purposes, he leads them in fact to further their purposes. He builds them into an organization to induce them to join in the common endeavor of public education.

But before we examine how the administrator of today's large-scale educational activities "uses" his community and associates, we can note also how the organization he builds also acts on him. Unlike the potter who does what he pleases with his clay, the administrator finds not only resistances he did not expect in the human materials he uses, but his materials also talk back to him; his materials—that is, the members of the school community—also have power generated outside the organization he is building; he finds that the statistically adequate answer fails to comprehend the particular situation; he cannot in many cases dismiss the exception as irrelevant. His materials are more than a mere passive condition of action.

More positively viewed, the organization's members also make autonomous and creative contributions to the administrative process. Not only might they offer effective resistances to being "used" by the administrator; they also play their part as specialists, for example, who bring to the undertaking meaningful contributions although they in turn receive from the organization (under the direction of the administrator) suitable inducements.

Our ideology may resist too bald a statement of the role of the administrator as "leader" and as "director" of the human partners in an enterprise; we need also to account for the fact of autonomous contributions of the members of the undertaking; "cooperation" may describe administration of the vast endeavors of education. Yet to gain new perspectives on the education of the administrator, we need to view him as the central figure in a process involving others as "his" instruments for the accomplishment of the aims of education.

These constructs move well beyond the familiar "policy" and "administration" distinction in that they allow us to view the school administrator as the key character in developing a "mix" of values, purposes, skills, ideas and ideals, people, and physical facilities out of which a school or a school system emerges. Rather than engage in largely fruitless speculation about who is "boss"—superintendent or school board, for example—or who really initiates the processes we call educational administration, we are beginning here with the conceptualization that views the administrator as the "hero" in the process. But like the Greek dramatic hero, he is in no sense free from challenges; he is in no sense assured of "victory" in every encounter with those whom the gods might have disposed to resist him; he does, however, make a difference in the outcomes of the action. He embodies the purposes of education. He devises alternatives and chooses means. He can probably only "muddle through," as Lindblom so aptly puts it, by means of a process of "successive limited comparisons" rather than by a grand single-minded pursuit of the larger goals of education. But it is no mere *tour de force* to choose the administrator as our hero, since both he and the people of his world acknowledge, even though grudgingly, the part he plays.

If the work of the administrator is even approximately as we have to this point described it, then knowledge of this work is, in the words of Simon, Smithburg, and Thompson, "knowledge of how to manipulate other human beings—how to get them to do the things you want to get done." They continue:

> The study of administration discloses techniques for influencing human behavior. To carry out a program of action the administrator is constantly trying to predict what the consequences will be of a particular course of action to act in ways that will produce the behaviors he desires and inhibit those he does not want. Only this distinguishes a realistic plan from a vague wish.[4]

Yet a key value in our Western society surely is that "human beings are not to be manipulated." How do Simon, Smithburg, and Thompson, along with the other "realistic" students of administration, take account of this value?

Within the framework of our own society, so-called "democratic" administration avoids part of the problem. If all the participants gain, in one sense or another, from the common enterprise, then administration is "cooperative" and no one is the victim of the evil purposes of the "boss." But, to refer again to Simon, Smithburg, and Thompson:

> There is little reason to believe that the harmony is complete. On the contrary, every administrator encounters situations where effective action dictates some infringement upon the desire of the individual not to be manipulated as a mere tool. He encounters many situations where there is conflict as well as community of goals—higher salaries to employees versus more economical service to taxpayers, for example.[5]

Consequently, the problem for the administrator moves to another level. No knowledge of techniques can relieve the administrator from the burden of making moral choices. And, his "code of ethics is as significant a part of his equipment as an administrator as is his knowledge of administrative behavior, and no amount of study of the 'science' of administration will provide him with this code."[6]

---

[4] Herbert A. Simon, Donald W. Smithburg, and Victor A. Thompson, *Public Administration* (New York: Alfred A. Knopf, Inc., 1950), pp. 22, 23.
[5] *Ibid.,* pp. 23, 24.
[6] *Ibid.,* p. 25.

The school administrator is thus under heavy strain. His ideology and that of his associates demands commitment to a "democratic" role; as he learns the nature of administration he confronts himself as a manipulator of his fellow men. How he steers a course here constitutes one of the "demands" on him that we will consider later.

To return to him in his role as administrator, we need also to go beyond Weber and note how purposeful school administration in fact is. The organization of our schools represents a primary commitment to the faith that change is possible. We postulate that men can, by taking thought, add to their equipment for dealing more satisfactorily with their world even though they may not thus add a cubit to their height. Even where the physical circumstances of the educational enterprise or the participants in it are variously resistant to change, we postulate an essentially optimistic view of things: the resources of science (i.e. knowledge), both theoretical and applied, can solve problems. Men are not fated to accept their lot but can, if they will, improve it.

Of course, we also often know better than we do. We are always falling short in one way or another; what we thought might be "solutions" of some problem turn out in fact only to help us identify further problems. Or, the solutions we invent may demand too high a price, as when the side-effects of a wonder drug limit its value. Out of all of this comes the fundamental rationale of what we call administration. For change is not only possible but nothing in our world stands still. Administration is the name we give to the effort to gain on our ever-proliferating problems. By definition our gains remain relative; if we seek a final equilibrium, the effort is hopeless. We deny nirvana by the very act of administering. The administrator is purposefully involved in an infinite regression.

Yet the administrator is not in our view on a treadmill. Even though he makes decisions of limited rationality, he can construct strategies of action that are progressive. He does help to move the enterprise of education in directions that he has identified as valuable. He is not simply driven by random forces but acts to relate means to ends. He intervenes to achieve some outcomes he selects, even though unanticipated consequences also flow from his actions and may sometimes even vitiate his highest hopes.

44

Part of the strategy of the administration rests on the fact that the administrator can identify and put to use many kinds of "feedbacks" from those whom he endeavors to change. His task consists in this respect in a kind of ordering of what might otherwise be merely random and unintelligible experience. Indeed, we call the process administration again precisely because it takes the measure of a policy in a manner analogous to the testing of, let us say, the strength of some structural part in a machine. "Does it work?" is a fairly straight-forward question in the testing laboratory. It is, of course, an endlessly more complicated question in the administration of the schools; moreover, the answers to it are not as clear as in the case of establishing the "breaking point" of a structural part. Yet we can properly picture the work of the educational administrator as continually putting policies to the test, as reshaping them in view of what the test brought to light.

As this kind of "feedback" gets put to use, the administrator reformulates and communicates outward to "his" organization the intelligence that supplies direction and dynamic for further change. No simple picture or pat analogy will serve to make wholly clear this equally complex process. As we probe more deeply what we mean by administration as purposeful change, we can think of the administrator as himself much like a teacher, the whole process of administration as education. As "teacher" in this circumstance, he may devise some of the underlying strategies and may communicate them to his "students," the participants in administration. He is often in control of the timing of the process. He makes some of the initial selections of what goes into it. But the outcomes in the changed behaviors of those who are the "students" quickly get beyond him. Yet his role is crucial, and in the model we are describing the administrator as "teacher" is ever re-establishing his initiative as he gives order to the "feedbacks" from the learnings of his "students."

Moving a step further, we may also usefully depict the participants in the processes of educational administration. They and what they command are resources for disposition by the man in charge, the administrator, as he mobilizes sufficient inducements he gets the participants in the venture to contribute to its goals. To one participant he might offer such inducement as profes-

45

sional advancement, sociability, or salary. For this purpose, the other members of the organization are to be conceived as means serving the end of inducing that participant to make his contribution.

The administrator, for example, may have to conceive of the legislature that provides funds for teachers' salaries as a resource to be tapped in order to serve the purposes of professional excellence in the schools. But the contribution of the teacher that he thus secures for the educational endeavor constitutes the means by which the children of the community are educated. Once educated, the young people of the community serve the end of inducing legislatures to make necessary funds available to the schools. But essentially, from the standpoint of the administrator, the people who take part in the process are instruments, means, resources. And as such he "organizes" them for their parts in bringing about the changes in behavior that are the end of educational administration.

The relations among participants in an organization is another means which the administrator uses to achieve his ends. For example, the participants bring their skills to the undertaking. Some of these may be technical, as those of the engineer, the lawyer, or the teacher. These might be conceived as "units" to be ordered like the parts of a machine. In the division of labor of a school organization, identifiable units of various skills can supply the bases for the decisions on the program; they are the "premises" of choices to be combined as the administrator uses the organization.

The organization may also be viewed as having the capacity **to compel and persuade those** whose behavior it seeks to modify. For example, through the organization the administrator may be able to offer curricula that use the best of learning theory to teach quickly and well. The organization may thus persuade by the force of its intellectual discipline. It may apply severe sanctions as through compulsory school attendance laws. We may view it as a structure for winning consent and assess it as a more or less effective tool for overcoming resistances to change on the part of those whom it seeks to educate. But such an abstract statement of the means the organization supplies for the administrator must not obscure how these same means may become the ends of the administrator's efforts—for he also seeks their "education."

Biological and physical processes and the related technologies may supply another perspective for viewing the means at the disposal of the administrator. At his peril, for example, he disregards facts about communicable disease if he hopes to maintain the physical health necessary for learning. Sequences of events ordered by casual relations in the physical or biological world provide the administrator with capacity to control outcomes when these are managed by an engineer. While we could develop countless illustrations of the impacts of growing scientific knowledge and technology, it is more important to note that in this context it is rather the people, who carry and communicate this knowledge, who give the administrator access to it as part of the premises of his decisions, who are the means of action.

Another view of the resources (and, of course, also the limitations) that need assessment as means for educational administration can be examined under the analogies drawn from communication systems. People can be viewed as they function to carry messages. Others perform in ways to "interfere" with communication like static on the radio. Still others perform systematically to amplify or enrich messages. Some transmit and others receive. Indeed, elaborate generalizations and empirical studies of organizations as communications systems may yet enlarge our understandings of administration.

Institutions and leadership relevant to processes of education can quite properly be conceptualized as additional means by which the administrator modifies the behavior of those who are to be educated. Barnard noted how the formal description of organizations ought to include the "customers." Only a modest extension of this thought urges us to examine the constellations of institutions and their leaders through which the educational administrators carry on their activities. We already noted the legislature and its relevance for access to needed funds. Other institutions with political and economic goals of their own often are in one or another special sense means to ends of education. For example, the business concern which employs the high school

47

graduate thus may serve as a means to an end of education. In another sense, the educational administrator also needs to view those who make up these peripheral institutions as ends of the educational venture. Their education needs also to be advanced if they are to serve as means.

We can abstract from the participants in the educational process markedly personal elements and also treat them as means to the ends the administrator seeks. Friendship, for example, or respect and admiration are often thought of as debased when viewed as means to ends beyond themselves. We speak with little sympathy about those who have ulterior motives in using their friends to further their ends. Yet to be able to count on one's friends constitutes for every administrator a resource that he uses over and over again, if only, for example, to speed communication by building on the widely shared premises that serve to join friends in a community.

Finally, to illustrate one more base on which to build our concepts of the means the administrator can use, we might note the great variety of statistical formulations about the characteristics of our world. These are, of course, abstractions about people and the way they conduct themselves. Yet we know with increasing assurance that statistical treatment of many crucial matters allows the administrator to manipulate his world. The physicist makes forecasts on the basis of a statistical analysis that tells him how many neutrons he will need to release in order to hit a given number of nuclei to make them split and release other neutrons to hit other nuclei, and so on in a chain reaction. So human behavior, regularized under statistical analysis, can likewise be brought under meaningful control, can become a means for administration, as when an administrator projects various population trends to determine the course of a school building program or the need for classes for exceptional children. Even as etymology indicates, it should perhaps be recalled, statistics has to do with the needs of the state and so of administration.

Here then is what we begin with in approaching the education and training of school administrators. These men and women need to be conceived as shaping those who make up the education enterprise, as using them to modify behavior of those who are to be changed in the process of education. The administrator is at the center of a complex set of interactions where "policy" and "administration" cannot be meaningfully separated. At the same time, because he is at the center of our study we conceive him mainly as using the organization as a resource; he cannot but be limited by its limitations, affected by its characteristics, moved ahead by its capacities, in a never-ending process of moving from the solution of one problem to another.

The Demands on the School Administrator

The description of the school administrator set forth above can serve as a conceptual mirror gathering light from often obscure and distant aspects of the work of administrators in real life. It may serve as a way to attend to what might otherwise be overlooked; it may also enable us to construct a clearer view (although in this paper at a fairly abstract level) of the demands that school administrators confront. And as these are identified we may be able to assess our resources for educating real-life administrators, particularly in the universities where professional education is these days ordinarily begun and brought to a formal conclusion.

When he made his first report on the findings of the Hawthorne Plant investigations, Elton Mayo pointed to a radically pessimistic fact: ripe for revision was the optimistic notion of the followers of Frederick W. Taylor that an administrator really only beat out time for the organization. Rational economic man, moved by simple calculations of net advantage, responding to inducements to tangible gain, of course, never existed. Yet much of scientific management in the past and many a large-scale organization, even today, operates as if he did. In Marxian societies no less than our own, Lenin's ideal of administration as "mere accounting" keeps many from understanding the processes by which the work of the world gets done.

Durkheim and Brooks Adams supplied Mayo with texts for proposing what the tasks of the "new" administrator consisted in. On him lay the vastly demanding burden of knowing his society. Vastly demanding, first, because as Durkheim came to see, industrialization and urbanization had torn people, as it were, out of society itself. *Anomie* confronted the administrator with a world

49

in which familiar reference points, foundations for conformity and so for prediction of the conduct of those whom he would affect, were seriously weakened. Vastly demanding, second, because as Brooks Adams observed, the number of new factors to be generalized had increased with the geometric progression of technological change while the capacity of men to generalize suffered as education responded to the pressures for more and more highly specialized training for a world of increasingly refined divisions of labor.

The brilliant insights of Durkheim and Adams have today received the support of telling testimony of many varied observers. They tell us of the rootlessness of people, their profound anxieties, their withdrawal from the society they find incomprehensible. At the same time, those who administer our affairs are required to keep in view and relate to each other such an array of incommensurables that their decisions appear to depart ever farther from rationality. How can the administrator reconcile or adjust the varied partial but competing and conflicting interests of people with a stake in his decisions? How can he know the probable outcomes of proposals for action when he cannot even assure himself that the relatively objective factors, the technical "facts" in the case have been accounted for?

In a close-knit, tightly integrated society, perhaps where status is ascribed, those who administer the affairs of a community have, as it were, a ready-made "theory" for describing the largely fixed relationships among those whom their administration affects. The administrator can refer his choices to a largely known framework of cooperation and conflict. By contrast, those who describe our society today (and they treat it from many points of view) lay out for us maps drawn to different scales, maps even without legends to let us know what the scale and markings on them mean. But they are not at fault. The world of changing relationships they seek to capture in their accounts cannot readily be reduced to single simple terms. And so upon the administrator falls the growing burden also of shaping the "theory" by means of which to conceive his community in order to forecast the consequences of his actions.

The demand to know the society comprehends also knowing

the meaning of the incredibly rapid rate of change in virtually every aspect of contemporary life. Our instruments that measure change, unfortunately, do not explicate its meaning. Moreover, so much change, so quickly, touching so many of the familiar landmarks numbs us. Take any index that tells of change: population growth, urbanization, energy available, inventions made, speed of travel, new products on the market, books published, students in school, TV viewers, or any of perhaps dozens of others. The numbers these measures tell us about quickly lose their meaning as they get beyond the range of our experience. Except in the grossest terms, the administrator cannot grasp what it means to accommodate twice or three times the urban population he once knew. What capacity do any of us have to attach meaning to even one megaton? Only the crudest meaning can be attached to, let us say, billion passenger miles. Yet these are all measures of the facts of contemporary life. Knowing them requires the administrator to give them meaning.

In all of this we demand also that our administrators make fewer and fewer mistakes in their decisions. At least two facts require an ever higher "batting average" of those to whom we look for direction of our common affairs. On the one hand the chain of indirect consequences of an administrative action has visibly lengthened. In John Dewey's terms all of our administrators' decisions have become more public as their consequences ramify more widely beyond those who are direct participants in them. As these widespread effects of decisions reach outward, the stakes in the administrator's decisions become larger and larger. He acts increasingly at his peril if he fails to perceive what may flow from his choice. We can tolerate fewer unanticipated consequences as these affect in such profound ways the workings of our integrated and interdependent social machinery. The history of the planning of the Los Angeles freeways and the consequences (too many unanticipated) that flowed out of the execution of the plans provides a dramatic illustration of what can be multiplied in virtually every field of endeavor. The costs of errors mount so rapidly as they burden ever larger numbers of us that we demand greater and greater mastery of the situation by our administrators.

51

Errors become less and less tolerable, too, as we find ourselves threatened by new and strange outside forces—the Soviet Union, the new nations of Africa, the "revolution of rising expectations" in the less developed world, to name just a few of these external threats. In educational administration, perhaps above all, we sense the compelling fact that we have dwindling surpluses, as it were, to draw on to cover our errors. We can suspect that many of our educational administrators whose incapacities and failures we could tolerate in an earlier and easier age will no longer meet our needs. The costs of wasted resources, unrealized talents, misdirected efforts of teachers and students, and most of all, the uncertainties of purpose and direction in education—these are practically unbearable when the issue is survival.

The demands on the administrator grow larger in view of the fact that he is increasingly not in control of the circumstance about which his decisions are forecasts. We know, for example, how the scientist in the laboratory constructs his forecasts of outcomes, either by holding constant significant factors or by disregarding them as random or in a sense universal conditions. In his "laboratory" the school administrator faces an "experiment" where his very act of forecasting (deciding) changes the conditions of the experiment and so confronts him in fact with unanticipated alternatives. Nor can he fully identify those factors that are sufficiently random to allow him to dismiss them in making his choices. The society—the very material of his "experiment"—does not stand still but contributes new factors to be reckoned with. And finally, the stakes in the outcomes are personally valued by those who are the subject-matter of administration. The "wait and see" approach of the laboratory hardly proves practicable when the "laboratory animals" prove unwilling.

Nor dare we overlook the moral burdens of administration. Our ideology often obscures the great costs of power to those who wield it within the framework of our democracy. We maintain the myth that no one ever rightly seeks power. Those who do must, we believe, share something of the qualities of George III or the French kings, indulging themselves freely and, of course, pleasurably, at the expense of the rest of us. Actually the heavy price of power needs a clearer analysis than our ideology allows.

Included in the price of power, as already suggested, is the burden of errors of great consequence. Included, too, are the impossible choices where the "public good" does not emerge at all. For these decisions the "science" of administration provides no answers. But a special fortitude is required to shoulder these demanding tasks.

The issue is hardly the "right" of the administrator to exercise power or, what comes to the same thing, to manipulate others. Power is rarely any gain for those who direct the work of our schools. Indeed, we recognize the high costs of power in many occupational fields—in business, for example—and provide rewards for the administrator there that are enormously greater than in public education. Our "best" people may find these rewards too attractive to continue to carry the burden and meet the costs of power in school administration.

What we need now is further clarification of these demands on the school administrator. We need to frame them so that the social scientists may be required to bring more of their knowledge into active use for school administration. In a sense, school administrators require education that enables them to satisfy both the need to know and the demand to do. These two do not always fit together. Yet our science must somehow make them fit.

We value highly achievement and success, and these are attained not in study and reflection but only in noisier and perhaps more public behavior. We are probably still so close to the image of the "self-made" man who left school at the age of twelve and proceeded to conquer his world that we are uncomfortable with the idea of long training, continuing education, intellectual discipline. We would not know quite what to do, for example, with Plato's regimen that kept the guardians in training until they were fifty. This would certainly be fiddling while Rome burns. But the alternative of action uninformed by the highest order of knowledge will, we can almost surely predict, fail to put out the fire.

These brief reflections on the demanding and, in fact, tense world of administration confront us squarely with the question of the character of the new perspectives in training our school administrators. If virtually everything about our society needs to be known, needs to be ordered and tested, needs to be acted on by the administrator, how can such a demand be met?

EDUCATION FOR SCHOOL ADMINISTRATION

Having taken the school administrator as the focus of our discussion and noted the demands on him, in what new perspectives may we conceptualize the processes for educating the administrators? We need to ask, first, how to associate selection with education. At many stages in the formal educational processes, we mean by "education" also the choosing of those who are to enter upon, continue, or complete the processes. The various formal assessments in education are intended to be cumulative. They are relied on at each succeeding stage of education *as if* they rested on values and methods universally shared by those who use the assessment. For example, the high school diploma certainly represents an important selection. But selection for what and on what basis? When a university faculty member relies on the high school diploma, his purposes may rest on premises not shared with colleagues in the high schools. Or, again, the teacher of political science is apt to complain about the troubles students have with their native language even though his colleagues in the English department have certified them as qualified in composition.

To choose men and women competent for the work of administering our schools we rely heavily on the colleges and universities. We can probably even make out a case that those whom the institutions of higher education identify as "superior" are good risks for professional training. We do not often ask, however, whether our colleges and universities choose these successful students at the cost of rejecting too soon those who could also have been successful or even more successful. Of course this is no simple problem. The reasons why some fail to make the grade in higher education have scarcely received any attention in the face of what seem like overwhelming and increasing numbers of those who do. Admissions offices and registrars often know a good deal about those who make it, but far less about those who don't.

We sense only dimly that we may in fact already suffer from

54

serious manpower shortages. The numbers of university and college students grow so rapidly that we readily assume that we have an abundant or even unlimited reservoir of the "best" on which to draw in selecting those who will administer our schools. But we may be facing a relative shortage, if not an absolutely limited supply, of people from among whom educational administrators will have to be chosen.

From another point of view, it may be useful to ask how the selection processes that evaluate the individual in higher education can also reckon with the fact that the future administrator succeeds or fails in a complex system of relations with others. Even the use of the term "school administrator" may overstate the plight of an individual alone in a hostile world that he has to master in order to succeed. We may see in this label "administrator" only a kind of lone operative in behalf of educational administration. But selection processes may need to take account more fully of the administrator *in* the organization; it may be only *in* the organization that the superior man can succeed in educational administration. Instead of the object of scorn he has become, the "organization man" may need to emerge as the goal of the selection mechanisms that operate in higher education. We may once more with Aristotle need to see the fulfillment of man in the associations of the larger organization, even in the state.

It is really, however, when we come to examine how the life and the logic of the university operate to affect those who finally are selected for educational administration that we face some even harder questions. Laying aside for a moment queries about the extent to which higher education can and does modify its students' central and deeply entrenched attitudes and characteristics of personality, what can we say about the bearing of higher learning on the task of liberating men from ignorance? How are the universities and colleges freeing the energies and capacities of men and women to take on the demanding tasks of administration?

In an important sense, these questions relate to the fact that the university, over the years, has often drawn back from inquiry into critical policy issues. Perhaps those in the university concluded that society could not tolerate inquiry into its public policies. Perhaps an age that let its fears and anxieties support a McCarthy could extend no sanctuary to the scholars who might criticize policy directions and methods. Perhaps for scholars to propose innovations in policy or experiments in social controls seemed folly or treason. Perhaps the professors rejected any part in policy-making. Perhaps policy-makers repudiated the professors. It is, at any rate, reasonably clear that "science" and "policy" do not mix well. In the social sciences the most prestigious work is not centered on large questions of public policy. The rewards of the academic enterprise for students, too, do not usually accompany concern for public affairs. Professors render their "public" service without necessary or intimate connection with those who are the centers of policy decision-making.

All of this affects profoundly faculty and students in the higher educational enterprise. All of this bears at once on those who move from this enterprise into the work of administering our school systems. We could now raise a host of questions designed to trace out all of the linkages between these factors impressionistically reported here and the educational outcomes reflected in men and women who are selected in this process for educational administration. But these involve necessarily detailed and carefully controlled study to help isolate "causes" and relate them to their "effects."

Only very superficial observation is needed to conclude that few specialists find energy or interest to relate themselves, their research, their teaching, to the world in which the school administrator will work. Is it too much to say that many a specialized student rejects knowledge of his own culture as irrelevant because his teachers before him have rejected it? Not two worlds, as C. P. Snow complains, but probably a dozen or more remain effectively dissociated in American higher education although evidently related in a host of ways in the world of public affairs and administration.

In the social sciences, against this more general background of the larger problem, we can discern the chief issues for school administration around the questions of relevance. Eleven years ago, at the annual meeting of the American Society for Public

Administration, John Gaus queries: "Who has better direct access to experience in and with government than the administrator and the scholar whose field of study is administration? . . . The administrator not only is entitled, but has a responsibility because of the unique access to technical experience and to the ways of people affected by large-scale collective action, to be making a greater contribution to social science generally." Gaus thought he could see in the Society productive patterns of cooperation among "a group of practitioners and scholars with administration as their central interest," and who view "administration as the essential constituent of any social theory that has purpose other than decorative."

To many in academia, however, action as a required outcome of research may even have a dangerous sound. Can our investigations not find ways to admit the administrator into partnership with the scholar to carry out social inquiry? Can our educational leaders help identify the common stake of both in knowledge and action? Perhaps a new John Dewey is needed to note and order these relationships. We need to inquire into the values that policy-makers, teachers, and researchers may share. How can they achieve mutual access to one another's worlds to enable such exchanges of experience and insight as to establish viable links between advances of knowledge, the training of scholars and administrators, the identification and resolution of the almost terrifyingly complicated issues of public policy?

Consider also how far apart are the world of the scholar pushing outward the frontier of knowledge and the world of classroom instruction. Little enough dialogue seems to take place between those at work in the laboratory and the teachers in the classroom, even on the same campus. How much do our text books reflect new knowledge? What share do teachers in elementary and secondary schools have in the work of social scientists? To establish communication here we often lack the organizing principles to make social science meaningful. Is not this a challenge to the leaders of our schools of education?

The loss is double when new knowledge diffuses slowly. New generations of scholars and teachers fall behind. But the researcher, too, loses a test of relevance. He needs above all to have put on him the demand to become intelligible to those who will follow him. He needs to be required to put his methods and and findings into "public domain" in the classroom, lest we suffer the tyranny of scholarly guildism and closed professionalism.

But as self-study in the social sciences focuses on a more suitable structure for the university undertaking, what is more urgent than to establish equally a more intimate dialogue between social scientist and policy-maker? Here, if anything, communication is increasingly incomplete. Here the professional training centers have a role to play.

Of course, the administrator uses the work of the social scientist. Witness Stuart Chase's record of use in *The Proper Study of Mankind.*[7] Many a social scientist offers himself and his work to men of affairs. Witness Alexander Leighton's *Human Relations in a Changing World.*[8] The methods of social science continue to "work" in the "outside" world. Witness the chief industry of Madison Avenue.

Yet the dialogue is far from complete. Nor does it consistently endeavor to advance the needed quest for larger knowledge. Policy-makers often are naive, albeit enthusiastic users of social science. Too often the "expert" in social science appears like the management consultant who offers the latest gadget to his customer. Policy-makers and scholars appear virtually to reject one another's premises and so they preclude access of each to the other. Perhaps the aggressive anti-intellectual bent of administrators in recent years can be connected with a fear lest they lose face by appearing not to grasp their tasks. Perhaps the social scientist senses a threat in "directed" research on terms not his own. Once more, the "brokerage" of the schools of education may invent the methods we require for a new pattern of relations.

Whatever analysis may bring to light as the university looks at its social science, it seems clear that we face a double need. Administrators require the most completely organized intelligence our science can produce. Gadgets are not enough. Wisdom without science will not yield good policy. The social

---

[7] *Op. Cit.*

[8] Alexander Leighton, *Human Relations in a Changing World* (New York: E. P. Dutton, 1949).

scientist needs the test of relevance from action. It may not be enough to know that administrators will buy his science; he must also discover how to enable them to frame crucial questions for social inquiry. Unless the social scientist finds how to communicate with the administrator we lose in not getting the most out of the scarce talents of the trained investigators.

Until some of these issues get into the life and habit of the university, until some of those who administer our educational enterprises learn to act in concert with social scientists, we will have to confess that we have no base for new perspectives on the tasks of training school administrators. The demands we make of them will continue overwhelming, and the intelligence we muster for the numerous battles against ignorance will fall short for want of the largest, most inclusive, and boldest strategy. We have not yet known how to deal with "applied" social science. It poses problems not comprehended within the patterns of relations, let us say, between nuclear physics and nucleonics. These relations—and they center in the university—involve developing new ties between theorist and user of social science. In these, of course, those concerned with professional education of administrators also have a profound stake. Here then may develop precisely the joint effort that Gaus hoped would bear fruit more than a decade ago. The hope may now once again be voiced as the schools of education enter upon the scene.

Chapter IV

Purpose-Defining: The Central Function of the School Administrator

JAMES G. HARLOW
Dean of the College of Education,
University of Oklahoma

The principal emphases of the recent past in the study of administration and in the training of administrators—that is the emphases of the last forty-five years—have been placed on the concept of basic process in administration, on organization or structure in administration, and upon human relations in administration. Most recently both in training and in research, there has been a very strong emphasis upon the concept of administration as the name for the interactions of a group of closely interlocking social roles. In research, a substantial intellectual effort has been directed toward the design of models of social interaction through which to describe social roles and their interactions in educational enterprises. The recent past in the training of educational administrators might be described as the period of rise of empirical description of administration, lately coupled with research effort to develop theories which can provide filing systems for the data already collected and direction for the search for new information.

This activity is familiar to students of the history and philosophy of science: it is the line of development along which the human mind has moved as it achieved today's powerful grasp of our physical and biological experience. As this developmental line, borrowed from the natural sciences, has been adopted and consciously exploited by the social sciences, we have gained new insights into problems of social structure and individual behavior—insights which have yielded and are continuing to yield new techniques and new opportunities for improvement in the quality of the organizational life of schools.

However, virtually all of the recent efforts at scientific description of structure, process, and interpersonal relationships in educational administration have neglected the pervasive effects of purpose in organizations. Perhaps this is as it should be. As workers in the natural sciences freed themselves from teleological pursuits and began the painstaking aggregation of fact which is both public and replicable, humanity emerged from individual and social dependence upon ritual and dogma and began the advance which today maintains our amazing lifespan and high levels of material living. For the last five hundred years, workers in the natural sciences have sought diligently to avoid asking questions about the purpose of the structure and processes which they seek to understand, and this effort has certainly been fruitful.

In matters affecting education, however, there is real question concerning the validity of an effort to avoid discussion of purpose—and this question appears with great brilliance in any discussion of training programs for school administrators. For public, wide-scale education is not a given in any social order; it is a creation. It comes into being as the servant of social purpose. Its content and processes are altered to accommodate changes in those purposes. And education itself bears most intimately upon the formation and revision of the purposes which it in turn is required to serve.

It can readily be argued that it is differences among purposes of enterprises which produce the enormous differences observable among them. The concepts of division of labor, for example, and administrative process, for another example, are as applicable to the organization and operation of fire-fighting groups as they are to schools. The actual modes of operation of the two enterprises at first glance are so dissimilar as to suggest that there is no common denominator connecting them. But, on certain occasions, a school looks very much like a fire-fighting group, as, for example, when it is conducting an emergency drill to train its members in processes to be used in case of fire, tornado, or nuclear attack. In its training periods, a fire company is much like the school.

What changes a warm-hearted, permissive elementary school into a tightly disciplined, rigidly defined set of behaviors upon the sounding of a specific signal? This is a moot question; it depends of course upon the definition of "school." The question precisely exemplifies the point to be made here—that the shift from learning process to processes for the protection of human life in emergencies is a shift in *purpose*. The people remain the same, the school building remains the same. But the purpose of the enterprise changes suddenly; and in this change of purpose there are born whole new modes of organization and process.

The purpose of preservation of human life, which must be a part of the purpose of every school, is a relatively easy purpose to develop among prospective administrators and is relatively easy to express in organization and in process. But the original purposes for which the school was created are not those of preservation of physical life. They are a different set of purposes altogether, purposes which are literally intangible, often difficult to express effectively, and difficult therefore to communicate to prospective administrators.

Administration is the servant of organizational purpose. Purpose pervades an organization, determining its subordinate and superordinate roles, its governing role expectations and the like. Division of labor and administrative process are determined by organizational purpose. It therefore follows necessarily that one of the principal emphases in the training of educational administrators—possibly the critical emphasis—must be placed on training in educational purpose and in the processes through which such purposes are defined. No amount of empirical description of schools or management, regardless of frame of reference, can supply the insights necessary for this task.

The need for formal, explicit, and extensive training in purpose and purpose-definition for educational administrators can be developed from another set of considerations arising from current organizational structures of schools. Consider the organization chart for the typical high school. A school group may range in size from a half-dozen to perhaps more than a hundred adults, engaged in what is presumably a single task, the education of the young. The group is featured by a very short chain of command. There is a chief executive, typically one or two assistants to him, frequently a small core of special staff usually called counselors, a few middle-management people called department heads or chairmen, and a very large group of relatively independent workers. In a school, the chief executive's span of control frequently is as high as thirty-five, and in spite of the strong departmental organizations found in some large high schools may exceed even that number. The main academic business of the school usually is carried on through a chain of command of two or three levels: teacher and principal, or teacher, department chairman, and principal. Counselors and assistant principals usually stand in staff relation to the principal.

The teachers are characterized by high levels of training—as compared with workers in other kinds of organizations—and by a tradition of great independence of action within their various individual spheres. In the upper levels of the public school activity, this tradition is reinforced by the typical teacher's high degree of specialization in training, a specialization which renders him relatively independent of detailed supervision by his superordinates. As with any worker, each teacher develops a considerable control of his own situation through detailed knowledge of the situations and the materials with which he works; in schools, this natural control is enhanced by the nature of the principal material with which he works, other human beings. It is indeed a brash principal or supervisor who moves swiftly into a classroom with detailed suggestions for an experienced teacher.

In enterprises featured by short chains of command and very highly trained personnel, the principal dependence for effective co-ordination must be placed upon shared purpose. Production (e.g., the learning of individual students) is maximized in the elementary school when the second grade teacher and the sixth grade teacher are following the same goal, when their institutional and personal value systems are congruent. In the secondary school, production is at peak when the teacher of physics and the teacher of English agree substantially about the contributions to be made by the high school.

Again, the need for training in educational purpose and in the processes of purpose-development emerges as a critical element in the development of the effective administrator.

64

Yet another line of observation and reasoning leads to the same conclusion. A superintendent or principal is not a free agent, though the mythology of education often urges the contrary view. He is not free to move his school in any direction which appeals to him, regardless of his sophistication and his skill in interpersonal relations. He does not "set policy." As a matter of fact, both the areas of action and the amount of movement possible to any educational administrator are sharply limited. He cannot replace his board. He cannot make wholesale changes in staff. He cannot alter the training programs through which teachers come to him. He cannot swiftly alter the outlooks of the teaching staff itself. He cannot sharply alter the pattern for commitment of funds within his budget. In short, the successful and highly contributive school administrator becomes so through the cumulative impacts of numerous small decisions, for he is permitted to make relatively few large ones. It follows that his success and contribution might well be predicted through measures of his own purposes, his awareness of those purposes, and his ability to relate his daily burden of small decisions to achievement of those purposes. The prospective school administrator must exhibit sophisticated purposes, must be intellectually aware of those purposes, and must be sufficiently committed to them that they actually control his day-to-day work with his board, with the other members of his administrative group, with his teachers, his students and their parents. Again, it becomes clear that training in purpose and in purpose-definition must be a significant part of the formal programs for prospective school administrators.

Even the nature of our times argues strongly for explicit and continued attention to the training of administrators in purposes and purpose-setting. The observation that ours is a time of extremely rapid change has become a cliché—but it should not be forgotten that clichés emerge to describe situations which are so conspicious as to be widely noted and commented upon. It recently has frequently been observed that the new task of the school is to train young people for living in a world which no one can yet describe—an observation which again brings to the very forefront of discussion that ancient question, what knowledge is of most worth? For, in a situation characterized by rapid changes in international relations, in material conditions of living, in the intellectual horizons of much of humankind, and in the understanding of the nature of our physical universe, the imperative for education is to be found in the determination of those purposes, those value systems, those behaviors which can be urged upon our youth, hopefully, in the deep desire to help tomorrow's adults survive the tests of their times. The fact of rapid change in our society, however, has not yet been reflected in the training of prospective educational administrators.

In the symposium, *Administrative Theory in Education* Professor Talcott Parsons[1] argues powerfully that educational organizations are so different from others that it is virtually impossible to reason from other types of organization to effective educational activity. In his famous *Democratic Administration,* Ordway Tead[2] some years ago argued much the same thing. John Dewey's writings have consistently held the same position; it cannot really be argued that those responsible for training school administrators have not had purpose-definition urged upon them. But formal training in educational purpose and in purpose-definition in programs for administrators remains limited to brief contact with the history and philosophy of education, and receives a typical commitment of about one-tenth of the course time of the graduate program.

One of the more curious features of the landscape of educational discussion of recent years has been the emergence of the term "value judgment" as a frequently recurring element. This term has, relatively speaking, been absent from discussions of administrative training for many years. It appears now most frequently as an epithet indicating intellectual contempt. A vigorous argument can often be won by the timely assertion, "That's just a value judgment." Apparently, this ploy has become standard in educational gamesmanship.

This use of the term "value judgment" is traceable partially

---

[1] Talcott Parsons, "Some Ingredients of a General Theory of Formal Organization" in *Administrative Theory in Education,* Andrew W. Halpin (ed.) (Chicago: Midwest Administration Center, University of Chicago, 1958), pp. 40-72.

[2] Ordway Tead, *Democratic Administration* (New York: The Association Press, 1948), 78 pp.

to today's scientific emphasis, which hopes to limit the areas of human action in which value judgments must be developed; and it is due in part to a lack of knowledge of the history of value judgments and of the processes through which such judgments are rendered sophisticated and dependable. The fact is that the human race has spent far more intellectual time and effort on value judgments than it has on scientific research. Our delight with our recently acquired scientific methods has caused us to forget the remarkable contributions of our older intellectual tools. We have behaved much like the home workshop addict who buys a wood-turning lathe and for years thereafter turns out nothing but projects which involve spindles.

Neither the democratic way of life nor the Communist way of life is the product of a scientific study. The decision to establish and maintain a system of public schools is not the result of scientific investigation, and the purposes to be served by those schools are not determined through scientific investigations. An individual's decision to marry and to rear a family is not a science-based decision. Our regard for each other and our ways of demonstrating that regard are not products of empirical study and analysis through symbolic logic.

Values and value judgments are the central elements in the selection, extension, and day-to-day realization of educational purpose. Purposes for schools can, perhaps, be inferred from the society at any given time, as for example, the use of colleges and universities as marriage marts for the offspring of our upper middle-class and upper-class population, or the use of the local high school to provide entertainment for the community through athletic contests. It is the choice among socially-urged purposes which is difficult, complex—and non-empirical. Who will say, certainly, on any basis other than probable employment survival of the administrator, whether it is better in the long run to operate schools and colleges as public entertainment agencies or as intellectually oriented activities and, if the school is to serve both, what makes an appropriate "mix"? This is the kind of choice in which the administrator must be both skilled and sophisticated; the kind of choice-climate in which his daily work is done.

In times like these, the determination of educational purposes is not a matter simply for an exercise in group dynamics. Neither is it a platform for the exhibition of a persuasive and charismatic personality. It is a matter for the most carefully reasoned, most carefully disciplined intellectual effort. It is in this fact that there is to be found an opportunity for the improvement of training programs for prospective educational administrators. For values and the making of value judgments are the domain of one of the major modes of human thought; namely, the humanities. These are the human studies, those which deal with the peculiarly human features of our experience. Actually, the sophisticated formation of value judgments requires a search for first principles, principles from which conclusions can be precisely derived. It requires study of the current and historical experience of all sorts and kinds of human beings exhibiting many sorts and kinds of value judgments. It involves the careful, rational development, explication, and evaluation of social structure and social process designed to realize value systems and to provide a fertile ground from which even more prescient, more sophisticated values can develop.

The academic names of the fields in which value skills and knowledge are developed are old-fashioned names so far as school administrators are concerned. If to improve education, we must speak in terms of discontinuities with previous experience and established knowledge, then there is little that this part of this paper has to offer. If, on the other hand, we can use older knowledge, perhaps there is a useful suggestion here. For, to provide effective training for prospective administrators in value-setting and purpose-definition, it probably is not necessary to create a host of new courses and programs, though some will undoubtedly be necessary. Most universities strong enough to train administrators offer courses at good levels of sophistication in ethics, in esthetics, in history and in general philosophy; and they typically offer courses in the history and the philosophy of education. Nearly any university provides a base for a good "mix" of materials and techniques in these basic humanistic fields. Good courses in literature are available in every major university.

Foreign travel, highly desirable for the correction of parochialism and ethnocentrism, is not a part of the graduate activity of most institutions. However, courses in the history and current practices of cultures other than our own occur widely among universities, though they are not uniform from institution to institution.

Even without the obvious contribution of contact with other cultures to the prospective administrator, there is opportunity in effort directed toward definition of basic content in the humanities for administrators and in the development of new collations of materials for training prospective administrators. And there are contributions which must be made to the selection of administrators, if genuine skill in both the modes of thought characteristic of empirical studies and modes of thought characteristic of the humanities are defined as desirable for a practicing school administrator. Historically, skill in these two kinds of thinking has not very frequently been developed to high levels in the same person. The established differences among the natural sciences, the social sciences, and the humanities are as much differences in tastes for intellectual activity as they are differences in content. It is interesting to note, however, that the recently developed aesthetic criteria for theoretical analysis in the physical sciences have begun to attract to those fields larger numbers of individuals who exhibit strong interest in and taste for such activities as music and drama. Today's physicist is much less likely to be a man with wrench, hammer, and coils of wire than a man with oscilloscope, jeweler's screwdrivers, highly developed mathematical skills, and hobbies in classical music.

Perhaps, if we set about seeking them, we could find for school administration equivalents of today's top-flight physicist, men and women with a grasp of empirical techniques in the social sciences, sensitivity to and skill in theoretical constructs, promise in human relations skills, and real awareness of and participation in the rich human endeavor to discover not only what is, but what is of most worth.

Perhaps we should begin to plan for conferences among humanists deeply concerned with education, presently active and prospective school administrators, professors of education, and university administrators in an effort to define humanistic content appropriate to the administrator's purpose-definition function.

Perhaps we could design and initiate working conferences to plan instruments and processes for selection of people who might develop the strong purpose-orientation, aesthetic tendencies, and practical skills suggested earlier.

Perhaps some universities could undertake tryout of behavioral sciences-oriented programs, plus follow-up contact and study as individuals move through the early parts of their administrative careers.

Perhaps support could be developed for really sophisticated and demanding in-service seminars, short courses and workshops in the humanities, designed for working school administrators.

In summary, the proposal here is essentially for division of the graduate work of the prospective administrator into three components of approximately equal size: (1) empirical social sciences, (2) humanities, and (3) technical management skills, culminating in the doctor's degree. Parenthetically, one could well argue against the continuation of the doctoral thesis in the Ed.D. program for administrators, substituting for it an internship of one year, following the medical school pattern, though this sort of arrangement certainly is not central to the argument of this paper. Discussion of reorganization of social sciences content and management skills content has been purposely omitted from this statement because the current literature is so rich in these fields.

Efforts to describe and define the role of the administrator, whether he be department chairman, principal, superintendent, college dean or college president, industrial executive or military officer have proliferated during the past fifteen years. Insofar as the educational administrator has been described, his role clearly encompasses many things. But among these things none stands out with greater clarity than the function of purpose-definition, the function of seeing that the purposes of the enterprise are accurately and explicitly defined, and effectively held up for view by the group.

It is not that the administrator must "set" the purposes. He must know what kinds of intellectual processes are involved in the generation of purposes, he must know what kinds of questions are significant in the development of purposes, and he must be informed as no other member of the group is informed, in the history of human purpose. The United States can no longer afford the simple group addition of assertions such as "I feel that . . . ," and "I believe that . . . ," and "I am convinced that . . . ," as a way to define purpose in so significant a group of institutions as its schools. It is unrealistic to hope that all members of a school staff can be equally proficient, equally sophisticated and equally interested in the problems of setting and maintaining institutional purpose. Purpose defining is the unique intellectual province of the school administrator; train him for it, we must.

Chapter V

Complexity, Specialization and Professional Knowledge: Overall Strategies in the Preparation of School Administrators

DAN C. LORTIE
Lecturer and Research Associate,
Harvard Graduate School
of Education

It is too bad that few of us can have faith in the prognostications of palmists, astrologers, or gypsy teacup readers. Some kind of revealed truth would come in handy as we try to select the best preparation for school superintendents. But it is unhappily and unavoidably true that any scheme of professional education is based on guesses about the future, as it is there that the graduates will either succeed or fail. I shall begin by giving my guesses on the future of the superintendency. I am certain that those of you whose grasp on the occult is firmer than mine will correct any misreading of the signs and portents.

We possess a presumably rational technique for forecasting, however, in the projection of trends which have, heretofore, shown great strength, and which apparently maintain their potency.[1] Perhaps the most striking feature of the superintendent's role is the movement toward greater task complexity both within the school system and in his relationships to the wider community. Overall management of the schools has become more complex as the kind of people who work and study there have become more diversified; such internal differentiation affects

---

[1] I wish to acknowledge the assistance of Dr. Janet Giele in the development of this section. Thanks are also due to Dr. Jane Roland for her helpful work on the nature of professional knowledge.

all aspects of administrative action. External relationships are more complicated because the broader society itself has a more intricate web of organization—today's superintendent must cope with a more demanding and potentially confusing set of interests and groupings. Such complications are apparently linked to general social change, and if this is so, there seems little chance that the future will bring a simpler superintendency. Our leading social commentators almost universally agree that the rate of social change will increase in the decades ahead. Does examination of schools—on the levels of policy, administration, and instruction—support or weaken this general forecast?

Educators may disagree on what part the superintendent should play in the setting of policy, but no one denies his key role in implementing school system goals and objectives. Yet this very implementation is problematic and will probably become more so with accelerated change. Larger school systems (the inevitable outcome of fewer school systems and the population increase) will entail greater reliance on bureaucratic methods of organization. Formulating "rules" which meet organizational and policy needs will require unusual sensitivity to all aspects of the school system and a subtle grasp of their interrelationships. As formal schooling plays a greater part in preparation for more and more occupations and hence affects the distribution of chances young persons have for rewarding or unrewarding lives, public concern with school operations will likely take on new intensity. Our relatively recent concern for psychological "goods" —a rise in the psychological standard of living—will mean new standards for assessing the performance of school leadership.[2] These examples point to what I think is already apparent—almost everyone has a bigger stake in what happens at the local school.

The basic issues that underlie questions of school policy are never resolved in any permanent sense—we must continually redefine the specific expression of our basic values as we meet new contingencies. "Equality of opportunity" or "excellence" or "separation of church and state" are not phrases which point to one clear-cut and indisputable set of administrative decisions.

---

[2] David Riesman points to this change in various writings. See, for one, *The Lonely Crowd* (Garden City, New York: Doubleday & Company, 1953).

Even if one such value involved no ambiguity, administrative decisions would still call for choice of one value over another. Perceiving and choosing will become harder as lines of authority lengthen and diversify. Long chains of inductive and deductive reasoning will be required if our superintendent of the future is to give reality to cherished American goals. To achieve integrity will necessitate philosophical sensitivity and analytic sophistication. Living with such demands will call for the capacity to perceive ambiguity and yet act with decisiveness.

Greater size, internal differentiation, and accelerated social change will have profound effects on the administrative aspects of the superintendent's role. Larger administrative units will lead to more layers in the administrative hierarchy, with the result that the chief administrator will look down from a greater distance on the place where the work actually gets done. More and more he will have to make assessments and decisions based on condensations of the work reality. Reports, statistical summaries, rates of this and that, short briefings—these will replace intimate contact with teachers, students, and custodians. The chief administrator will need the ability to interpret and use abstractions, then, which symbolize the reality he must influence. Internal specialization will require administrators with minds able to grasp the special functions of each sub-unit and the ability to relate each unit (and the people in it with their characteristic and even esoteric viewpoints) to the whole. Again we note the intellectual qualities needed as he seeks to mesh each element into an effective whole. The difficulties introduced by change need no special exposition; we find increasing recognition that change calls for men who can think abstractly and imaginatively. Nothing wears out faster than specific solutions to specific problems.

The situation in instruction has been described as an incipient revolution. We can see the accuracy of this depiction in shifts in teacher training and staff utilization, in the introduction of new technologies of machines, programming, and television. Established curricula are melting under the advances of science in both nature and the affairs of men; new concepts in architecture (necessary because of instructional changes) make ten-year old buildings look old-fashioned. Revolution in instruction will, of course, introduce effects in every phase of school administration and call for a multitude of new decisions. But the revolution is just beginning if we believe the forecasts made by scholars. The amount of substantive knowledge we can expect to be produced in the next twenty years will flood not only universities but public schools which, historically, have always inherited a proportion of the advances in knowledge.[3] How will future school leaders go about the painful yet crucial task of selecting from this vastly increased body of knowledge? The answers they give to this question will have much to do with the culture we transmit to an entire generation of Americans.

This brief overview of the demands that will face future superintendents should be enough to show that their leadership qualities must be rooted in intellectual ability of a high order. Our task is clear, if not simple. We must identify and attract men with high native capacity, assist them in the development of their gifts, and provide them with the knowledge that will make superior performance highly probable. This job is difficult enough, I believe, to require our willingness to get the best guidance we can in establishing a system of professional education equal to the challenge.

Although the superintendency calls for a "mix" of personal qualities without exact duplication in other occupations, we can find some important similarities between requirements for it and for other socially crucial positions. The superintendency has much in common with the older professions—a central similarity is the need to combine intelligent thought with effective action. It is, of course, an old American habit to model new, would-be professions on those which have arrived, but such imitation, sometimes based simply on the wish for higher prestige, is often an unselective aping of features of marginal importance. To learn successfully from older fields, we must concentrate on basic solutions to general problems, and we must make unhurried adaptations that take full account of the specifics of the newer occupation. Lack of knowledge constantly hampers such efforts, but it seems that we often know more than we are willing to use.

---

[3] See John S. Brubacher and Willis Rudy, *Higher Education in Transition* (New York: Harper and Brothers, 1958).

Professional preparation in such fields as medicine, law, engineering, and architecture is similar in one key respect—the division-of-labor established between university and profession in the induction of new practitioners.[4] For in each instance, that division-of-labor rests on the recognition that the education of the young practitioner is *not* complete when he graduates from professional school. Receiving the diploma is but the beginning in a series of major turning-points in the learning career of the doctor or lawyer. The man who wants professional recognition faces several subsequent junctures where he must show his competence and face either acceptance or rejection by those judging that performance. Senior colleagues watch juniors with a complete lack of sentimentality; law partnerships or major hospital appointments are not assigned to men with minimal credentials. Such credentials merely define the pool from which candidates for major responsibility will be selected. The specific arrangements for teaching and testing young practitioners vary from field to field, but they are of crucial importance in all the older professions. Professionals learn the values of their profession in the early years of practice along with numerous tricks of the trade; it is during this period that they are sorted out by their elders as men to watch or to ignore.[5]

The division-of-labor between university and profession, then, is one where the university's function is to *begin* the professional education of the practitioner-to-be. The nature of the professional school itself reflects this limited though important function— we note it in the curricula, faculties, and student bodies of leading schools of medicine, law, engineering, and architecture. All these point to an emphasis on the creation and transmission of general, systematic knowledge relevant to the practice of the profession. Only limited attention is given in these schools to many values

---

[4] The same division-of-labor is found in other professions as well, as in the ministry, the armed services, and some schools of business administration. My research into education in twenty professions suggests, however, that the four mentioned here have more in common in this respect than fields with shorter histories or radically different social functions.

[5] These comments apply, of course, to professional work done where colleagues work together, as in hospitals, law firms, architectural firms and groups of engineers. They do not apply to the less-disciplined efforts (technically speaking) that are found where these professions are practiced in isolation from colleagues.

and skills the student must learn to become a full-fledged member of his profession.

The curriculum of the professional school in well-established fields usually includes the sciences and disciplines which are considered basic to the profession plus the body of organized knowledge developed in the field. Medical schools illustrate both types of general and systematic knowledge in their combination of basic sciences (e.g., biochemistry) and professional courses (e.g., surgery). Yet the student will learn few of the skills he would need actually to perform a major operation; such skills are learned later, if at all. Faculties in leading professional schools are composed increasingly of substantive specialists whose major commitment is to the university and its efforts. The core faculties of leading professional schools consist of men with orientations and careers similar to those in the historic disciplines, and they share the same ideal of advancing knowledge through research and are fully aware that their reputations depend on their contributions to knowledge. But such men are not all alike in the kind of research they do, and the differences have great importance. Some are men with deep involvement in basic science who care relatively little about the application of knowledge. Others, however, contribute to the profession by ordering and developing knowledge which is not only systematic, but also relevant to improving the administration of justice or advancing the state of architecture. If the knowledge found in professional schools has any distinctive quality, it is this feature of *relevance* to the problems faced by practitioners.[6] A word only about the students in such professional schools: they are young, rigorously screened, and involved full-time, for several years, in their basic schooling.

If the university omits so much in the preparation of its students, how are effective engineers, lawyers, doctors, or architects produced? It is here that the profession itself—in activities at the work place and in its professional associations—plays the

---

[6] The knowledge produced by such men seems to have another unifying characteristic—it presumes that the learner is interested in how his intervention can make a difference. Perhaps the vitality of some of the leading professional schools comes from the interaction of men with these different orientations to basic versus applied knowledge.

vital role. The medical internship and residency are widely known, but other well-established professions also rely upon arrangements which are, if less formalized, very similar. The early years in the architectural or legal office are largely training years; beginning engineers usually play limited roles on important projects. These young men become "professionals" in a process where they apply the general knowledge they have acquired in school to a series of gradually expanding assignments carried out under the supervision of senior colleagues.

There are at least three ways in which this post-academic learning differs from university instruction. It is "real." It involves genuine responsibility for others. It is under the control of experienced and successful practitioners. The reality comes from the fact that the young professional is *acting,* not studying or observing or replicating in some variant of the Link Trainer. The element of responsibility stems from the fact that his skills are applied to persons who are ill or to constructing buildings which could fall apart. It is this element of responsibility, perhaps, which makes the supervision of senior practitioners so important and which underlies their niggardly assignment of tasks—the young man must be carefully taught and assessed if the profession is to avoid public censure for irresponsible work.

The testing and learning done on the work premises are supplemented by the activities of professional associations. These activities range from elaborate and formal systems of specialized instruction and examination (e.g., medical specialist certification) to informal help such as special courses, lunchtime seminars, and so forth. The meetings of the older professions frequently achieve a level of scholarly discourse that would do credit to a learned society; the regular journals pour out results of investigations to those who can use them in daily practice. The details are less important, however, than the major point that these professions have developed a highly effective machinery for building and diffusing their professional cultures. This serves all types of practitioners but is, of course, of special importance to the beginner. The diligent neophyte can, through taking advantage of the opportunities available, shorten his learning by reducing the amount of trial-and-error he must personally undertake.

Those in the university, the work place, and the professional association, then, each play a vital part in producing effective and responsible practitioners for the older professions. What we see are the many advantages of specialization as men of different abilities contribute their special knowledge and skill to beginners. The academic man produces and communicates knowledge that has broad applicability; practitioners sensitize the neophyte to the uniqueness of each situation and instill suspicion of the glib generalization. Professors influence students to identify and reflect on their basic assumptions; practitioners teach the short-cuts that make it possible to get the job done. Professors discourage students too lazy or inept to master complex matters; practitioners advance those who prove that they can meet professional standards under the stress of working conditions. The various parties can fight for their emphases because they know other viewpoints are getting effective expression. It is this condition which permits a healthy and creative tension which the serious beginner can come to terms with and integrate in himself. Equipped with conceptual discipline and a burgeoning set of practical skills, he selects what impresses him as valid and develops his unique professional style.

Specialization, moreover, need not imply separation, for as each educational component defines and refines its contribution, cooperative mechanisms become possible. The work of research scholars can affect practice and be effectively molded to fit reality as new graduates press recently developed theories on older practitioners. A new synthesis results as the theory of the young is coupled with the insights of the experienced. Practitioners can press their academic colleagues to work on troublesome problems and curb academic inclinations toward the esoteric. Brilliant practitioners, proud of an ingenious solution to a vexing problem, can report it to colleagues and see it incorporated in academic instruction.[7] What is impressive to me about prepara-

---

[7] In this age of science, it is easy to overlook the basic importance in professions of the contributions of working practitioners. Law is, after all, produced in courts and legislatures. Any textbook in internal medicine is replete with medical discoveries and treatment developed by practitioners. Unless such innovations are recorded, however, they never become part of the general culture of the profession.

tion in the older professions is that *as systems,* they create, hold, and transmit a great variety of knowledge, skill, and values. As systems, they incorporate the relevant basic science, applied science, and professional experience. The culture of these professions is the product of the several groups. It builds up through steady accretions of knowledge and skill acquired by men in diverse situations. This culture, since it is recorded, is available for those beginners who have the drive and the seriousness of purpose to learn it. Men learning how to become members of the profession are exposed to diverse ideas and diverse people. It is this diversity, I believe, which gives such professional cultures their richness and their observable impact on the young professional.

We need not judge ourselves too harshly if professional preparation for the school superintendency has not attained the level found in fields with longer histories and greater affluence. But if the superintendency is becoming more complex and crucial to our society, we cannot afford to luxuriate in self-congratulation. To do even an adequate job in the future will probably require substantial improvement over current efforts. Our position is not without its strains. We are in the same position as a manufacturer who must reorganize his entire company while maintaining regular production. We face similar dilemmas in how to use scarce resources to achieve the long-run aim of building a first-class educational apparatus while simultaneously preparing men for the immediate future. Before I present some suggestions on how we might resolve this allocative puzzle, however, I should like to sketch out, very briefly, the kind of apparatus I think we will need in the future. I shall do so in terms of university, work place, and professional association, and although I would not agree to put a date on when these features can be expected, I should not be surprised if they came much sooner than any of us would dare predict.

The curriculum of the university program of the future will be broader in scope, more specific in content, and more firmly rooted in scientific evidence and modes of thought than any we can offer today. Policy matters will be examined both in terms of ends (examined with philosophic rigor) and means; means will increasingly come under the sway of input-output analyses which involve measurements of outcome and the rational selection of alternatives in terms of such measurements. Such analyses will involve sophisticated use of automatic data processing; the students will have acquaintance with the necessary tools and logic. Students will be expected to understand the social, political, and intellectual heritage of the schools and will study monographs prepared by leading scholars. Problems of a more narrowly administrative type will be set against a background of theory just beginning to develop today. Such theory, based on empirically sound propositions, will allow students to design specific types of social structures for specific purposes. Technical aspects of the administrative role—business management, school law, plant design and maintenance, personnel selection, financial planning—will be taught with materials based on the school reality but with concepts partially derived from other professions and disciplines. Students will examine critically (they will be carefully prepared in statistics and scientific method) the studies of learning and related problems of instruction; they will become expert in tracing the steps between overall objectives and specific plans, and they will know how to measure the relative success or failure of one set of instructional arrangements over another. The entire curriculum will lack automatic answers as students are forced to think their way through problems in each area and are trained to think for themselves. Materials, drawn from reality in the schools and the community, will be ordered and conceptualized in ways it is not possible to anticipate today.

The faculty found in such programs will be highly diverse. Men steeped in history, economics, philosophy, political science, sociology, will do scholarly studies of schools and school problems and communicate their perspectives and findings to administrators-to-be. Such men will have colleagues, however, of equal brilliance but of different viewpoint. These will be "scholars of the practical" with special expertness in areas such as facilities, staff organization, public relations, finance, who will bring research abilities and analytic minds to various facets of school administration. Their publications will break new ground in the major problem areas important to chief school officers. They will, of course, be well-informed on what is happening in the schools, but they will not spend any appreciable time giving service on local, idiosyncratic problems to individual school systems. Such a use of their time would be wasteful as it would compete with the broader contribution they have to make to the entire profession. Service work to schools will be done by men of less genius in creative research but of high skill in the solution of immediate problems.

If such programs emerge (I believe they can), they will have little difficulty in attracting the ablest, most idealistic of American college graduates for the combination of intellectual excitement, involvement in the world of affairs, and the opportunity for public service is an attractive one to American youth. Students, studying full-time for two or three years, would develop an identification with the profession and, very important, a sense of colleagueship through their close association with each other. They would leave the university ready to learn the specifics of everyday administration and with a determination to raise the level of the entire profession. The sense of colleagueship, coupled with research skill and intellectual curiosity, would produce at least some men capable of making important contributions to clinical knowledge.

So much for the university. What should happen in the places where school administrators work? Here I suspect at least three major developments must occur if school administration is to reach new levels of excellence. First, the career of the would-be administrator will be carefully planned as school systems learn to work together. Men will leave the university (let's assume they are young but have taught at least a couple of years before their intensive training) and will follow carefully-charted positions leading up to the superintendency. They will be rotated through departments in large systems and will be employed as assistants to top administrators in several types of school systems. Superintendents will feel it is an integral part of their professional responsibility to give them carefully planned "on-the-job" instruction. Secondly, standards will become higher as top administrators can choose between several well-prepared men. Competition for the higher posts will allow greater choice and greater emphasis on the results produced by any individual. Third, research and development will grow and improve in quality as, I hope, schools realize the value of the careful recording of experience and the necessity for subjecting their experience to scientific analysis. Hopefully, schools will turn away from their addiction to the oral tradition and begin to put things down on paper; as this occurs, administrators on the way up will be intimately involved in the tough-minded assessments that will mark superior school systems.

The professional associations in educational administration have already done much to advance the quality of training offered in schools by insisting upon new requirements for membership and new standards for accrediting training institutions. The next major development, I hope, is that they will turn their attention to raising the standards of their publications and their meetings. These could become a major instrument in continuing the education of the young administrator. The content must attain new levels in order to satisfy the newer generation of highly trained practitioners. If school administration's associations follow the lead of their opposite numbers in medicine, law, engineering and architecture, we can expect them to become vast storehouses of practical knowledge and to be active in the scientific advancement of the field. Whatever one's assessment may be of the political action of associations in these older fields, we cannot gainsay the importance of the *technical* contributions they have made to their respective professions.

What strategy can we use to move the field toward this kind of educational development? I believe it is possible only if two things occur so far as the allocation of resources is concerned. First, we must apply the principle of thrift by the multiple use of scarce resources and by avoiding expenditures which do not serve *both* short and long-range interests. Secondly, I think we must expand our total resources if we are to do anything like the job that is mandatory. I should like to illustrate these two principles with a few suggestions.

In setting up our programs in the immediate future, we should select that instruction which will prepare well now and add to our resources of knowledge—perhaps the most important capital accumulation we can make. Reliance on social scientists for instruction in programs of educational administration diverts no energy away from long-range development if such men are expected, and given time, to do research. Experienced super-intendents can add much to the instruction of young adminis-trators and add to our long-range aims where they analyze their experience, give it general statement, and communicate it effectively. Students taking courses in other units of the university (be it the humanities or business school) can acquire knowledge needed in school administration in a way which makes the most of existing resources. Administration students will naturally take courses available in education which deal with curriculum, guidance, educational psychology, and the like.

There are two kinds of instruction, however, which I believe ideally suited both to the immediate instruction of students and to the building of clinical knowledge. The first is becoming popular—the use of cases in instruction. I wonder, however, if it is generally realized that cases can be more than an immediate pedagogical tool. The collection of cases by thoughtful professors can, through time, lead to exactly the kind of knowledge that is most directly relevant to the preparation of practitioners. Exam-ine the units of instruction in a superior law or business school, and you will find that even where there is the greatest insistence on the purity of the case method, a large amount of conceptuali-zation—shrewd and valuable conceptualization—has developed over time. Cases are organized under specific rubrics, and in the highly developed courses, each case is planned to teach a particular insight. The "notes" that accompany cases are often new orderings of knowledge that approach scientific levels of sophistication. The central point I want to make here is that cases can lead to a special kind of theory—theory which is organized around the perspective of the participant rather than the observer and, therefore, theory which can be of direct assistance to the practitioner.

The second type of instruction which can serve our double purpose is the administrative project carried out by the student after he has left the university but before he earns his degree. We have used such projects at Harvard for nearly ten years now and are beginning to see exciting ways in which they can con-tribute to the development of knowledge in administration, as well as to the increased administrative skill of the student. It is too early to talk of results, but we see no reason why bright students, involved in administrative responsibility and committed to recording and analyzing that experience, cannot produce pedagogical and even theoretically significant materials. There is further promise in this arrangement. If it succeeds, it may help to make future administrators see themselves not only as doers, but also as contributors to recorded knowledge in the field. If this hope is realized, we have made a definite addition to our capital resources.

A word or two should do so far as the work place and the professional associations are concerned. The development of effective in-service programs of training and the attempt to record and review experience need not await large appropriations. The cost here, for at least minimal programs, is time; where men are sufficiently convinced of the importance of improving the quality of administrator training, they can find that time. The professional associations may well be able to make noticeable strides without great infusions of cash. There is one contribution that practitioners could make today without enormous expenditure; they could attack the problem of how school systems can work together in internships and other areas—to overcome both the financial limitations facing many and the unfortunate parochialism that is all too prevalent.

Thrift, however, can take us only so far. If we need new resources, where can we invest them to ensure the greatest multiplier effect? What expenditures—assuming we could get greater support—would be the lever that would upgrade the preparation of administrators-in-training?

The best single investment we can make in the training of school superintendents is, in my opinion, the development of a small but superb cadre of men who will become the needed scholars of the practical. Men of original research talent, rare teaching skill, and deep commitment to the optimal performance of our public schools will not be easy to find; to create such a corps will take money, energy, and the sacrifice of some of our institutional myopia. I believe the price is well worth the product. With such men, a first-class system of professional education for the superintendency can become a reality.

What are the specific needs? First, we currently have too few men with special interest and training in the preparation of school superintendents. Second, our intellectual resources in educational administration are widely dispersed geographically and institutionally. Third, very few universities have special programs of study for men planning to teach and do research in school administration. The profession, to my knowledge, has no overall plan for the recruitment, selection, and education of professors of administration. Fourth, research in other fields is producing knowledge so fast that much of it, potentially of great usefulness to schoolmen, does not find its way into educational administration.

Should funds become available, we could devise a program of action that would meet these immediate needs and build toward long-range objectives. Interested universities could work out together some estimate of the number of men needed in the years ahead—I suspect the annual number would prove to be small. A nation-wide effort to identify promising candidates could be undertaken and full financial support be granted to those who are selected. The interested universities would then agree (hopefully) to accept a fraction of the number selected. Each student would receive the degree at his original institution, but his program of study would include time spent at other universities. This would not allow the student the gains of working with many different leaders in the field, but would make it possible for him to do research on schools in a variety of settings. Provision would also be made for study outside the field of education *per se*. A man interested in teaching school plant matters might spend some time in a school of architecture; the would-be finance man might want to do some extra work in economics or business finance. The central feature of such a program would be its flexibility and its scope. We could maximize present knowledge—wherever it resides—and produce men capable of producing new syntheses or new depth in their specialties.

The sociologist should probably leave to the administrator the creative work of developing workable schemes of action. This is, after all, close to the heart of the administrator's craft. I do hope, however, that as we consider ways to improve the instruction given to the superintendents of the future, that we will not overlook the need for instructors of the highest calibre and for researchers who will build that knowledge the superintendent will surely need.

Chapter VI

The Education of Educational Administrators

JOHN WALTON
Professor of Education,
Johns Hopkins University

Administration has long been one of the great practical arts. Today, the complexity of social organization, with its urgent demands for administration, and the modern faith in formal study as a means for the improvement of practice are responsible for earnest efforts to transform this intuitive and common sense activity into a science or a learned art. Generally, the study of administration has been divided according to the types of organizations to be administered; e.g., business, government, educational, health, military, and ecclesiastical, on the apparent assumption that administration is so intimately related to or modified by the substantive activities of organizations that it must be studied in their respective contexts. However, there is an opposing view: some students of administration have assumed that the administrative process is basically the same in all organizations. This latter view, modified by some consideration for the mores and substantive activities of educational organizations, underlies the recommendations in this paper for the professional education of administrators.

The assumption that the administrative activity is essentially the same in all organizations is admittedly controversial. However, the constant lament among educational administrators, that purely administrative duties consume their time, is a clear indication that organizations demand administration. Probably educational administration is in a transitional stage. As educational organizations become larger and more complex, the administrative function appears for what it is, and it resembles

89

very much that which is referred to as administration in other organizations.

This assumption does not preclude the possibility that the administrative activity must be adapted to the special demands of different kinds of organization. Although there are those who will ask, "Does not this adaptation, in fact, change the very nature of the administrative process," we think not. It is our opinion that the administration of public education should be viewed as a form of public administration, and public administration, in turn, as a form of general administration. Possibly the closest analogue for educational administration is the public administration of technical, scientific, or artistic pursuits. Looking inward, both face Daedalian substantive activities. Looking outward, both are confronted with the conflicting values of a pluralistic society; and both are concerned with the maintenance of organizations. It is, then, with the formal education of a special kind of administrator, rather than that of an educator, that we shall be concerned.

Before making any specific recommendations for the professional education of administrators, we shall consider rather briefly two questions that obtrude themselves when attempts are made to transform a practical art into a profession, a science, or a learned art. These questions are (1) How do we select and organize the subject matter that is necessary, desirable, or appropriate? and (2) How can systematic study make its maximum contributions to the improvement of practice?

Often, when the matter of professional training is discussed, the analogy of medicine is invoked. This tendency is understandable since medicine has been notably successful as a profession. Also, our frequent references to it may reflect the respect we have for a profession that exemplifies so many of our values— science, humanitarianism, and financial success—rather than any real similarity between medicine and education or administration. As a matter of fact, it is extremely doubtful that administration will ever become a profession like medicine, with its well-organized body of scientific subject matter. Nor is it like law and theology, which have ancient corpora of subject matter, traditions, and rituals, wherein the mysteries and the arcana are carefully guarded by formidable language. However, administration does have some subject matter of its own, and it can draw extensively upon the social sciences and the humanities. It is reasonable to suppose that this knowledge can be organized and taught in such a way as to improve the practice of administration.

In the selection and organization of the curriculum, we should be guided by (1) the duties and responsibilities of the administrator; and (2) the amount and quality of the academic subject matter available. The first can be determined by a kind of job analysis, but investigations of this kind should be broadly conceived and rigorous in their methods. Even a cursory look at the modern educational organization will give us some clue to the administrative task. Educational organizations have become so large and complex that they require full-time administrators. So urgent are the purposes of these organizations that education, once a somewhat peripheral activity in our society, now seems to be moving into the center of things; and the educational enterprise is now the focus of many major social and political issues.

Therefore, the educational administrator is now a full-time administrator of an important social institution, who must attend to the accomplishment of highly urgent and complicated goals in the matrix of social conflict. Through the maintenance of organization he is expected to provide stability and balance in the educational system and to insure the accomplishment of the accepted objectives of the schools. But he is also expected to discern the changing educational needs of society, the general goals which are unclear. Logically, his position as administrator does not provide him with powers of over-all policy-making, nor does it legitimize his role as the one who gives direction to change. Yet he is held responsible to some extent if the educational organization does not respond to the changing educational needs of the social order.

It is in this area of the formulation of organizational goals and purposes that the administrator's role is most ambiguous. The clarification of his responsibilities here would be of great help in determining the kind of professional education he should have.

The second criterion for the selection of the content of the curriculum for the education of administrators is the quality of the subject matter. Classes and seminars should be organized around topics for which there is enough respectable academic knowledge to justify such activity. It may be argued that classes and seminars should be organized around professional problems, regardless of the amount and ·quality of academic knowledge, since in this way we may increase such knowledge. This is doubtful. The facile solutions to the persistent problems of education and of administration, arrived at in gatherings of well-meaning pedagogues and experienced administrators, through common sense, shared experiences, and the mystical group process, may be consoling and helpful; but they have added little to systematic knowledge.

Certainly these conferences should be continued, but let them convene in seaside hotels or in temples erected to common sense, which has long deserved an institution. It is not the function of an academic institution to purvey common sense. To be sure, we should conduct research in all areas of education and administration, in those areas where knowledge is sparse as well as in those which have made considerable progress in scholarship. But research is a highly specialized activity in itself. While the curriculum designed for the education of the administrator should prepare him to understand and interpret research literature, it should not be designed to prepare researchers or scholars. The responsibilities of administration and scholarship differ, and the kind of people who are good at one may not be good at the other. In the professional education of administrators, we are not primarily concerned with the discovery of new knowledge, but with training personnel in the knowledge that we already have. Our curriculum is, therefore, limited by the amount of teachable knowledge available. The increase of this knowledge is the responsibility of the researchers and the scholars, of the men who discover and systematize knowledge, rather than of those who use it for practical purposes.

The second question we promised to consider is: How, in the professional education of administrators, can academic study be related to practice? In all learned vocations, including the scientific ones such as medicine and engineering, there appears to be an inevitable discontinuity between study and practice, between the analysis of action and the departure for action. In formal academic pursuits men tend to think with a view to other thoughts and to ask the question, "How is this thought or idea related to other thoughts and ideas?"

In practice men ask, "Shall I do this or that?"

Furthermore, study and practice occur under different sets of conditions and are accompanied by different kinds of consequences. This discontinuity between the two is reflected in the clichés, proverbs, and stereotypes about the differences between men of theory and men of action, between the thinkers and the doers, between the professors and the practitioners. It is true that practice may be inhibited by the tentativeness and prolonged reflection of scholarship; and scholarship, in turn, may exhaust its energies futilely with concerns for the immediate and practical. But it would be absurd to assume that the performance of administration, or any other practical art, would be hindered by a study of its problems. On the contrary, despite the discontinuity and often the conflict between the two, we may expect the study of administration to improve practice. All professional education is based on this assumption.

Let us look briefly at some of the ways systematic study may be related to practice. First, as has already been pointed out, professional education must select out of the vastness of organized knowledge the subject matter that appears to be most relevant to the practitioner's task. For example, a course in public finance, with some emphasis on educational finance, might well be included in the education of the prospective school superintendent. It should be no great problem to organize a number of respectable courses or seminars that have some significant bearing on the administrator's task. The greatest difficulty occurs in the process of relating academic knowledge to the decision-making of practice. The optimum conditions for doing so occur when our subject matter lends itself to a treatment such as the following: under conditions a, b, and c, x can be expected to result in y; or more commonly, in order to bring about y, do x. However, the practitioner must decide when conditions a, b, and c obtain, and whether or not he wants y. We may, in turn, help him to understand and to identify conditions a, b, and c, and to recognize the grounds of his valuation of y, but in practice he has to make the decision.

To say that subject matter of this kind provides the optimum conditions for relating study to practice is not to say, necessarily, that this is the most important kind of subject matter for the professional education of administrators. Other kinds of subject matter which may not be so obviously related to practice and which may provide only partial answers, analogies, and suggestions, may give insight into and provide perspective for some of the major problems that confront administrators. This is particularly true of problems arising out of the major social and political issues. But it is here that we run the danger of being pretentious, if not dishonest, in our claims and efforts. We cannot in academic study anticipate and offer pat solutions for all the problems of practice. To attempt to do so would result in a meretricious—both vulgar and spurious—practicality.

If the above paragraph appears to exaggerate the meagerness of the academic knowledge that can be related to practice, we shall seek to redress the balance by pointing out that, although administration is not a highly developed science, there is a great deal that can be taught about government, social organization, and administration that has great relevance for practice. For example, any detached view of the educational system reveals that it has become bureaucratized, and that, like Molière's famous character who had been reading prose all his life and was not aware of it, educational administrators have often become bureaucrats without realizing it.

Now there is a considerable folklore about bureaucracy that is often recalled and repeated without careful analysis. In addition there is a considerable body of systematic knowledge about bureaucracy, such as categories for description and classification; empirical generalizations about the relations of bureaucracy to the substantive activities of organizations, and to external pressures and controls; and schemes for analyzing and understanding organizations. The practitioner can be educated to bring to his work a kind of intellectual sophistication that he is not likely to develop under the exigencies of practice. Furthermore, there are means of relating systematic knowledge to practice. Teaching for transfer in an intelligent way and without straining for *ad hoc* applications is helpful. Also, through the case method, incident techniques, observation or simulation of administrative activity, projects, and internships, professional education can relate the two.

If we are to make sound progress in the education of administrators, the two questions which were raised near the beginning of this paper must be given continued and thoroughgoing analysis. However, in the recommendations which follow we approach the realm of practice in which one is forced to say, "Do this, or do that."

And if progress is to be made, a certain boldness is necessary. But in the reflective phase of this undertaking, we shall continue to ask, "How should we select the subject matter?" and, "How can it be related to the practice of administration?"

Our first recommendation is that all educational administrators, above the clerical class, should have a broad, liberal education, for which four years of undergraduate work is not too much. Educational administrators represent to the public the educational enterprise; their general education and cultural background should be better than that of practitioners in other professions. Generally, society has demanded that they be impeccable in morals; we recommend comparable standards in their general knowledge, their use of language, their reasoning, and their tastes. Honesty, common sense, and a host of homely virtues are necessary but not sufficient. The men that represent the educational enterprise should be men who are unmistakably educated.

Furthermore, we are justified in believing that a broad educational background in the humanities, the social sciences, and the sciences will provide perspective for the administrator in all organizations and particularly in those devoted to public service. He should have superb training in the English language; he should know a great deal about the social sciences; he should be aware of the nature and force of the natural sciences; and he should know how intelligent men have dealt, and can deal, with the persistent problems of justice and value. It is true that it is possible to acquire a liberal education without going to college, and many people who graduate from liberal arts colleges are not liberally educated. But the requirement of four years of general, liberal education would help insure a good academic background.

The question now arises as to whether we shall recruit the candidates for administrative positions directly from the ranks of liberal arts college graduates or from such graduates who have prepared for, and engaged in, teaching. If, as we have assumed, administration is essentially the same in all organizations, why not train an administrative class, the members of which would be interchangeable among organizations, or at least among those devoted to public service? We may expect this sort of thing in the not too distant future.

However, for the present, there are several reasons why some, and perhaps the majority, of educational administrators should have some teaching experience. For example, the fact that an administrator in education has taught gives him some protective coloration in an academic environment. But it is possible for an administrator to acquire some expertise in education without having taught; he can learn something about education in his training for administration. Therefore, some candidates for administration should be recruited from liberal arts college graduates who have not taught as well as from those who have. For the latter group a fifth year program in teacher education and two years teaching experience should intervene before they go on to their professional education in administration.

The professional study of administration, both for those who enter it directly from college and for those who enter via teaching, may someday be done in advanced schools devoted to the study of administration and public affairs. These schools will in all probability include courses and seminars in the substantive or intrinsic activities of organizations that will give the prospective administrator some acquaintance with such technical pursuits as public health, education, studies of geographical areas, scientific research, and so on; but this training will not be designed to turn out specialists in these fields. A high degree of specialization in the substantive activities of organizations is one sacrifice adminstrators may be expected to make. However, under existing conditions, the major responsibility for the education of educational administrators falls on schools and departments of education.

Therefore, it is suggested that the recently adopted practice of organizing the curriculum on an inter-school or inter-departmental basis be continued. Commonly referred to as "an interdisciplinary approach," this plan has great merit, but it should regard more seriously the two criteria for the selection of subject matter suggested above.

We now propose a curriculum for the education of educational administrators. Like all such proposals, it will provide only a general outline; the substance of the curriculum will depend on those who are responsible for it. Perhaps we can convey some idea of the general nature of the subject matter and the general intellectual orientation that appear to be desirable.

Curriculum

I

A few, perhaps no more than three, semester seminars in the social sciences: government, public finance, and social organization. The academician may ask, "Are these seminars to be at the undergraduate or graduate level; and, if at the latter, how can we be sure of adequate undergraduate preparation?"

The answer to the first part of this question is neither! These seminars should not be designed to train research scholars. Rather, they should attempt to provide the prospective adminstrator, who, we assume, is an intelligent, well-educated college graduate, with the information, basic problems, some of the methods of inquiry, and a general knowledge of the relevance of these disciplines for administration. The academic quality will be determined by the kind of subject matter that is introduced and by the intellectual level of those who deal with it. It is a curious development in the academic world that the question of academic quality is usually answered with reference to research standards. In our considerations here we should divest ourselves of this strait-jacket.

II

A year-long seminar in administration. This seminar should deal with such diverse matters as the use of computers and the use of power. A general knowledge of the former seems essential for the administrator today, to say nothing of the one of tomorrow; and the latter has been a problem since government began. Perhaps the great literature in which the use of power has been described offers greater insights than the research in the modern behavioral sciences. Selected readings from literature and philosophy could well be used. Also, there is a growing body of literature in the theory of administration, comparative administration, management, and the psychology of groups. Topics such as the social role of administration, the validation of value judgments, and the role of efficient management *vis-a-vis* education should be considered in depth.

III

A semester seminar in the government of education. Such matters as the organization of education in the United States, school law, and comparative studies in educational systems would comprise the subject matter.

IV

A year-long seminar in the literature on education. This literature should be selected to produce "the generalist" in education. It is unrealistic to expect the educational administrator to be an authority or a specialist in all aspects of education. He must, in his decision-making, rely on the counsel of specialists and experts. But he should know something about the development of education in modern societies; he should be aware of the great educational problems and issues and the answers that men have given; he should be familiar with the main outlines and results of the research literature of modern education.

Although it would be enormously depressing to anticipate the counting of credit hours, we may use the credit system as a rough measure of the program suggested. It would be the equivalent of twenty-four semester hours. This is enough, and perhaps too much, for one year of study. The notion of thirty semester hours credit broken up into ten or twelve courses in one academic year is ridiculous. No student can do first-rate graduate work in more than three or four seminars or courses, and graduate work demands full-time study.

During the second year of professional education the student would be engaged in more practical pursuits, either as an intern in educational administration, or in the completion of projects designed to solve practical problems. Both the internship and the projects should be under the major direction of practical men whose experience and intuitive judgment would be of more value than the knowledge of the academician, although the latter should continue to be responsible for scholarly information and research methods. As an example of a project, a graduate student in administration might be assigned to a study to determine the building needs of a large city school system and to participate in the decisions about where the buildings should be constructed. He might assist in a study and the subsequent decision-making about a major change in educational policy. Or he might work on a program for school district reorganization. In all of these projects he would be required to participate actively in solving realistic problems, and he would have an opportunity to bring to bear on these problems the knowledge and the insight that he acquired in his more formal professional study.

If the above recommendations are followed, the time required for the higher education of an educational administrator would include four years of undergraduate preparation, one year in preparation for teaching (for those who were expected to teach before entering administration), and two years advanced study for administration. If we assume that the administrator is to have two years teaching experience, normally he could complete his professional training at the age of twenty-six or twenty-seven. This would place him within the range of other graduate students, and it would relieve to some extent the problems associated with the education of mature, practicing schoolmen who are forced to give up their employment to attend graduate school. The financial problems are obviously serious, and there are more subtle problems involved in a mature, successful practitioner assuming the role of a full-time student. They may return later for conferences, institutes, and symposiums, but they would return as mature participants and not as suppliants for credits and degrees. As graduates of this program they would enter educational systems as administrators. Probably they would work in various aspects of administration; and from their ranks, school superintendents would be recruited.

Undoubtedly many questions will be provoked by these proposals. How will candidates for administrative careers be selected? What effect would such a program have on the teaching profession, in which the prospect for advancement faces almost entirely in the direction of administration? What effect would the establishment of an administrative class have on education and other professional activities and on society? We cannot answer these questions here.

However, we now select candidates for training in business and public administration, and the procedures we use may be improved as we learn more about the requirements of the administrative function. Teaching might become a career in its own right and not be regarded as a stepping stone to administration. Clearly, this development could enhance the status of teaching. A clearly designated profession of administration might improve the government of education and, at the same time, protect the substantive activities of the schools from the interference of administration disguised as education.

As for the general social consequences of having an administrative class in education, and thereby adding to the number and prestige of managers, if we are to enjoy the advantages of a highly organized society, we must be prepared to deal with the undesirable concomitant effects. We are already alerted to the dangers of bureaucracy, the loss of individuality in organizations, and what Burnham has called "the managerial revolution." We can control these hazards better once we have recognized the nature of and the necessity for administration.

In this paper we have based our recommendations on the assumptions that administration, as the execution of social policy, is an activity so important and complex that it can be improved by professional preparation; that education, having become institutionalized, requires the administrative function for the attainment of its goals; and that this necessity will become more urgent. We have not presumed to suggest solutions to other important problems that will arise. For example, it may be necessary to create or revive policy-making bodies, as an integral part of social organization. Also, some clear lines of demarcation and relationship between administration and the substantive work of organizations will have to be drawn in addition to deliberate measures to protect and encourage the freedom and the anti-organizational tendencies of creative individuals.

Since we can expect to live in a highly organized society, it does little good to decry the fact of organization. Rather, our energies should be spent in making sure that through the intelligent control of organization, as many of our values as possible are preserved. This applies to education as well as to all other organized activity.

Chapter VII

A Comprehensive Program for the Preparation of Administrators

THEODORE L. RELLER
Professor of Education,
University of California, Berkeley

The proposal offered in this paper pertains primarily to the preparation of administrators who will serve in the central or area offices of a school system. It is not designed for the preparation of elementary or secondary school principals. The central focus of the program is the superintendent of schools, with consideration also for other top public administrators in relatively large organizations. Many of those persons prepared through the program will serve on the staff or team of a central administrative organization prior to appointment as a chief executive. Some will remain in these positions.

In this proposal attention is given to three major matters. They are: basic assumptions regarding the society, the educational situation, and educational administration; the person who will be needed in the administrative situation; the program of preparation.

SOME BASIC ASSUMPTIONS REGARDING THE SOCIETY, THE EDUCATIONAL SITUATION, AND EDUCATIONAL ADMINISTRATION

The population of the nation and of the world will continue to expand at a rate which should be a cause of increasing concern. Furthermore, the increase in population will be located almost entirely in the metropolitan areas, many of which will become almost endless conurbations. The opportunities for youth to gain significant educational experiences through work for some economic return will further decline. A larger percentage of the population will probably have feelings of futility about the part which they can play in determining local and national policy. The sheer population numbers will make it more difficult to maintain belief in the worth and dignity of each individual. The pull toward conformity in many matters will increase.

Mobility of population both within the nation and in the world will continue to increase. Thus there will be more opportunity for peoples of various races, creeds, and ideas to exchange views with one another. The mobility will threaten the security of many groups and will cause some to seek segregation or isolation for "protection."

There will be fewer school districts. The approximately 40,000 in the nation may well be reduced to 5,000 in a couple of decades. The districts which remain will be large ones both geographically and in population. In the metropolitan areas new organizational structures will be developed. There will be either extremely large districts (in population), within which considerable decentralization or deconcentration has occurred, or another tier of government will be provided. The new tier of government will be a federal system of the districts in the metropolitan area. It will replace any intermediate unit. It may be a government of rather limited but of extremely significant powers. It probably will not directly provide or administer elementary and secondary schools. These functions will remain the responsibility of the primary units.

Education will be more closely coordinated or integrated with other services such as public health, housing, social welfare, land use, recreation, employment and assistance for youth, and library. The growth in population and the concentration of population with the attendant problems will require that education be related more significantly to the lives of children and youth and to other organizations which bear upon them. This integration may take place through coordination of the efforts of various governmental organizations or through some changes in legal structure which may facilitate a broad, common attack on problems.

The educational service will become a much more varied one.

This will result from the greater recognition of the meaning of individual differences and from the attempt of the society to attain variety and diversity to offset in part the growing tendency toward conformity. The confusion of identity and equality of opportunity will largely be eliminated. It will be seen that quality education even for the intellectually able is not attainable without much more attention to the social and cultural barriers to education which confront many youth. These barriers may be found in the home, the community, and in the subcultures within the school. They are found especially among the minority racial and ethnic groups residing in large numbers in the core cities of the metropolitan areas.

Equality of educational opportunity will be reexamined and redefined. The redefinition will recognize ability and application not only in matters of the intellect through traditional academic studies but also in areas such as literature, art, music, drama. This will be essential both to fulfill more adequately the commitments of a democracy and to maintain a position of leadership among the peoples of the world. This development may require even more attention to the home and community life of the child as it relates to the values, attitudes, and understandings which are brought to school and which determine aspirations. Many new frontiers will unfold with the realization that it is not equality of opportunity to make a provision and to assume that all children have equal or reasonable opportunity to take advantage of it. Even larger frontiers will open up with the realization that equality of educational opportunity must be provided in areas such as music, art, and drama.

The teaching staff will be characterized by differentiation. It will achieve higher levels of competence and through its organizations will have a larger role in the development of educational policies. Teachers will accept leadership responsibilities in the development of the educational program and in educational experimentation. They will have large responsibilities with reference to professional personnel policies and practices in the schools. They will also be more deeply involved in community activities, including political life. The social status of the teacher, which appears to decline with the development of education for the masses and with industrialization, will improve sharply because of an awareness of the growing dependence of the society upon education.

The involvement of large numbers of citizens in policy formulation will be more consciously sought. The role of the citizen will be more limited and sharpened as a result of more dependence upon research with reference to many problems. Public opinion will be more adequately assessed, and its limitations will be more generally understood. The role of the expert (his contributions and limitations) in society will be better understood. The services of the expert in relation to the people in policy decision-making will be more effectively employed. The citizens will consequently act on the basis of informed opinion. The closeness of the schools to the people will be sought or stimulated through decentralization within the local units of administration.

School systems will consciously be decentralized. In line with this policy the principal and staff of each school will be encouraged to develop, in cooperation with the people and other agencies of their school community, a school with a unique quality and life. The schools of a given neighborhood area will join in their efforts in this regard. The administrators located either in the central office of the system or in a divisional (geographic) office will be seen as the stimulating and coordinating agency through which planning, research, and educational development are carried forward. The system will concentrate attention upon securing a high level or quality of approach to problems rather than to uniformity in practice. Emphasis will be upon the identification and study of problems confronting the children and the school, to the development of programs in light of this study, and to evaluation of results. The central office (or its divisions) will provide stimulation and assistance in this effort and will encourage the coordination of the work of various schools and the coordination of the work of the schools and other agencies.

Research will command a far larger part of educational expenditure than is true today. Research and development will become the mark of the outstanding school system no less than it is the mark of the most promising industrial organization today. The stimulation, planning, and directing of research will become one of the major responsibilities of the chief educational administrator. Boards of education will seek men who have done significant research for appointment as chief administrators and, whether successful or not in that search, will insist upon their chief administrator's having high competence in the design and conduct of research. This insistence upon research competence will not be a substitute for the basic values, vision, professional commitment, and competence essential for leadership in a school system operating in a complex social setting. Rather, it will be a correlate of these qualities.

There will be many fewer chief educational administrators because of the decline in the number of school districts. There will be many more highly competent administrative staff members attached to the central office or to divisional offices of the system. These men will be engaged in the stimulation of research and in the coordination of the work of principals and teachers. They will also be involved directly in major research projects which involve many schools. Many of them will participate in group research projects. Many of them will need competencies not widely different from those of the chief administrator.

The central and divisional staffs will devote major attention to fundamental research and intensive study, in the light of which policy decisions may be made on questions such as: the program for youth provided by educational and other agencies; the place of technical education and its integration with humanistic, general education; the maintenance of desirable pluralism in the society through the schools; the part of the resources of the people which should be devoted to education; religious and spiritual values and education; the role of the changing home and community in education; the development of diversity through emphasis upon the unique features of individual schools; issues in administrative theory pertaining to administrators, staff, and citizens. In establishing policy regarding such matters, administrators will have a large role as policy is more largely determined in the light of research. Administrators may well regard their work along these lines as the most significant of all of their opportunities.

Superintendents of schools will increasingly be selected from those who have served in the central administrative (including research and coordination) service of the system or of one of its divisional offices or in a similar capacity in another system. The principalship will provide directly fewer of the superintendents. The superintendency of the small district will contribute fewer of the leading administrators because of the decline in the number of such districts and of their limited ability to provide the quality of experience which will be needed.

Educational administration will be recognized as a process which has much in common with administration in other large public enterprises. It will be apparent also that effective administration in education or other areas requires a thorough familiarity with the field in question and an awareness of its unique features.

The chief executive will remain, but responsibility for administration will be carried more largely by a team. It will not be regarded so largely as the prerogative of one man. Decision-making will be far more dependent upon research findings. The method of science will be employed to a sharply increased degree in working through problems.

The contribution of administration to policy determination will be recognized, but responsibility for basic legislation will be firmly placed on the legislative body. Within the broad framework of legislation both the central administration and the legislative body will vigorously encourage the instructional staff (teachers and principals) and the people to develop educational institutions which meet the needs of children and young people.

Those in the central and divisional administration service will concentrate upon the clarification of purposes and the facilitation and evaluation of their realization. They will accept the view that the strength of the system is dependent upon the strength (initiative, responsibility) of the units within it and consequently seek vitality and diversity within a broad framework. This they will do through leadership in research, assistance, and coordination. The maintenance of the system, an inevitable and essential responsibility of the administration, will be facilitated through the involvement of people in the realization of purposes rather than through activities which are maintenance oriented.

In conclusion it may be noted that educational administration is caught up in a changing world. Such forces as demographic changes, technological changes, increasing mobility, extension of communication, intensifying of contacts between diverse peoples, extension of governmental interest and action, and increasing value attached to research, operate to fashion a new setting within which the public school system must function. The new administrator must be aware of and be able to provide leadership within this setting.

THE QUALIFICATIONS OF THE ADMINISTRATOR

The administrator who can fill the leadership role in the society and educational setting described in the preceding pages will have need for knowledges and competencies well beyond (different from) those generally sought in the educational administrator heretofore. The closer relationship with other peoples of the world calls for new knowledges and abilities. The growing significance of education in various societies and the potential use and abuse of education by them raises questions regarding the basic values of our own society, of its subcultures, and of other societies. The changing education necessary because of scientific advance and the growing aspirations of people presents a new challenge. The approach to educational problems through a greatly expanded research effort while holding to the "traditional" commitment regarding the role of the people in policy determination brings important issues forward. A new concept of the educational statesman is indicated: one who is "at home" in more societies than his own; who sees the educational problems of his own society more clearly as a result of his knowledge of others; who is research oriented and competent but capable of evaluating the contributions of the research in a broad philosophical framework; who is a scholar; who is dedicated to creative leadership rather than mere manipulation; who sees education as a most important instrument in determining the kind of world which men will build; and who knows men, their needs, and organizations sufficiently to aid them in utilizing their potential power in a way becoming of the finest qualities of man.

Specifically, this educator will need a high level of competency (knowledge, technical skills, conceptual ability, human [leadership] skills) in the following areas:

109

1. The changing world and the forces at work in it.
2. Culture and education in societies other than his own—with strength in at least one other.
3. Historical and philosophical backgrounds and sociological conditions of his own society.
4. The local community, its composition, and the forces at work in it; community organization, how various institutions may cooperate in their efforts.
5. Human growth and development.
6. The processes of education.
7. The organization and functioning of formal education and its relation to informal.
8. Large-scale organization, theory and practice of administrative organization, structure, functioning in general (i.e., in other selected areas) and in education in particular.
9. The behavioral sciences and their contribution to an understanding both of the individual and of groups (large and small), leadership, power, authority, motivation, change.
10. The character and potentialities of research; research design, administration, and utilization as applied to a wide variety of issues in education and related areas.

The old argument whether the superintendent should be a manager, engaged primarily in the important control and direction aspects of his work, or a leader, contributing to the clarification and further refinement of goals and an aid in moving toward them though improving the quality of decision-making would appear to have less meaning in the future. As always he must meet both challenges but especially he must be a leader with a greatly enlarged vision of the potential of the education service and statesmanlike ability in leading society toward the effective realization of the potential. Further, the society with which he must be concerned must extend beyond the school district, to the state, and to other nations with which our nation will be cooperating.

The Program of Selection and Preparation

It is proposed that the program described here shall be a consciously planned university program for the preparation of public administrators. The program outlined here contains more detailed applications to educational administration than to any other area. However, the same basic program could be readily developed or adapted to other areas of public administration with appropriate detailed applications.

The program should be sharply separated from the general university program of graduate studies which has other purposes primarily in view. This does not mean that it should not utilize regular university offerings (in education or other fields for which the student is preparing) but, rather, that it should have a core designed specifically in light of its own purposes. It should be an entity and have a life of its own within the university community. It must be located on a major university campus which has strength in the behavioral sciences, education, educational administration and other fields of public administration, and in area study, especially in newly developing countries. The significance of this will become clearer as various aspects of the proposal are described.

It is, further, the view that this program should not replace the existing programs for the preparation of various types of administrators. Rather, it should be an experimental program utilizing some of the offerings of existing programs.

The program should be one for limited numbers of high intellectual competence and outstanding leadership potential. The number admitted to the program at any university in any one year should probably be between 15 and 30. It is proposed that they should be preparing for several different types of administrative situations. The situations for which they would prepare would be as follows:

1. For positions of leadership in educational administration in the United States.
2. For positions of leadership in other public services such as public health, public welfare, the city managership, city or county planning.
3. For positions of leadership in education and community development in newly developing countries.

Approximately one half of the students selected for the program should be preparing for administrative leadership in education in the United States. The remaining half should be divided somewhat equally between the other two categories. To be a member of this student group would be an educational experience of great value to all of the participants. They would develop a recognition of their common values and tasks. Those preparing for leadership in areas of administration other than education would focus attention on their respective areas of public service. The necessary coordination of education and other public services would be greatly facilitated through having those who will be leaders in various fields engaged in a common core program of graduate study. Those in each group would learn much about the unique demands of their respective fields and would carry a high level of cooperation into the field. There would be values as large for the noneducator group as for the educators through this experience.

Those preparing for leadership in newly developing countries would similarly not only gain a great deal through the program but would contribute much. They would stimulate interest in the newly developing countries and would thus contribute to aspects of the program itself. They and the study of their societies would bring to the whole group an understanding of the interdependence of education and of other services and of the relation of these services to the society itself. The newly developing countries constitute an excellent laboratory in which to examine the need for "balancing" education and economic, social, and political growth. The program might also make a large contribution to the newly developing countries which are in extremely great need of leaders who have the fundamental type of administrative preparation envisioned here.

The representatives of the newly developing countries would strengthen the area study aspect of the program—while engaged in an area study. Through this they would gain a knowledge of the values and problems of another society. The other society would throw into bold and at times shocking outline the nature and scope of many of the problems confronting the peoples of the world. This would enable them to look at their own society with clearer understanding. Values, power, large scale organization, administrative theory, decision-making, leadership, cultural barriers and conflicts may frequently be seen more clearly in one's own society through the lens of another society. The examination of administrative processes in different societies would also offer an excellent opportunity to explore the question of whether these processes are themselves a product of the cultural milieu. This aspect of the program would thus be readily justified in the case of all of the societies involved. It might also prepare a few potential leaders for service in societies other than their own—a contribution which more universities should be making.

With the above areas in mind and the general competencies and high leadership potential held in common, students should be recruited from the following sources:

(1) Educational administration: principals of schools, assistant superintendents, directors of services.

(2) Teachers. It is anticipated that relatively few would be secured directly from this source.

(3) Holders of the bachelors or preferably the masters degree with a major in one of the behavioral sciences. It is assumed that these people generally would not have taught. This is regarded as one of the more promising sources of candidates for the program.

(4) Public administrators: assistant city managers, assistant directors of planning, and junior administrators in various public service areas.

(5) Junior administrators and directors of services in ministries and provincial governments of newly developing countries. These men would be nominated by their respective governments and selected in cooperation with representatives of agencies such as foundations, the Administration for International Development, and The United Nations. Not more than two new enrollees would be accepted from one country in any one year.

Selection would be one of the most important tasks. It would be planned by those who would have major responsibility for the conduct of the program. Intellectual achievement, intelligence, and leadership promise would be important criteria for selection. Generally those selected for admission would be between the ages of 22 and 35. It would be assumed that those selected would spend a minimum of two years in the program with most of them devoting three to five years to it.

The program of study would have the following characteristics:

Core Program

The core program would be directed to the achievement of those knowledges, understandings, and abilities which are essential to effective administration in any area. They are presently not adequately developed in professional courses and are dispersed in a number of disciplines. The core program would bring them together for the benefit of the student. Other aspects of the program would provide for their supplementation and implementation.

The core program would be participated in by all members of the group. In the first year it would constitute 40 to 50 per cent of the program. Variations in the per cent of time devoted to it would be planned individually in light of the previous education of the students. In the second year approximately 30 to 50 per cent of the program would be core. This includes extended work in research design and understanding. In the third year roughly one quarter to one-third of the time would be devoted to this aspect of the program. In this year the core work would be fused with the work in the specialization and concentrated on research.

During the first year attention would be given especially to matters such as: basic values, cultural change, theory of administration, organizational structure, large and small groups, leadership, the role of the expert, the structure of societies (community, school, state), government, change, decision-making, communication.

The second year of this part of the program would be devoted to a continuation of concern regarding basic knowledges drawn from the behavioral sciences and to the planning and conducting of research. Intensive work in research design would be provided. During the third year the emphasis would be upon completing a significant research project.

During the first year the methods employed would be diversified. Case studies and simulated materials drawn from various fields would be used to bring reality to the teaching situation.

Lectures and mastery of the outstanding related literature would also be required.

As a result of this part of the program, all students should have a thorough knowledge of the contribution of various disciplines which relate to administration. They would also have a basic competence for research work in administration.

Area Study

Area study, as has been suggested, would be designed to broaden and deepen the individual's understanding of his own and other societies. It would also contribute to an understanding of other men and their values and thus establish a base for working with them.

Provision would be made for each student to develop knowledge and understanding of an "area." An "area" would generally be regarded as one (or more) of the newly developing countries. If in the case of any student more than one country is involved, the countries would be selected because of cultural similarity and geographical proximity. "Area training" suggests an exposure to the total context of the area concerned. Generally the student would study political science, sociology, education, community development, and anthropology concerned with the area in question.

This study would be concentrated largely in the first year of the program. The student would also spend at least one period of no less than three months at work in the area. In most cases the period of work in the country would be six months to one year.

The foreign students in the program would select for area study from the following among others: Puerto Rico, Jamaica, Mexico, a special area or group in the United States.

Special Field for Intensive Study

In the case of those preparing for leadership in educational administration in the United States this work would be selected from among the offerings of the department of education of the university. Through this offering a comprehensive knowledge of education would be developed and an understanding of those aspects of administration and the related technical skills which are unique to education. Those students who are preparing for leadership in other areas would similarly develop their specialization program from the regular offerings. In this way they would secure a comprehensive knowledge of their field and the unique aspects of administration in it. The foreign students would generally select from a somewhat broader field in light of their special needs.

Work in the area of specialization would extend throughout the duration of the program. Course work would be pursued in the first and second years with the third year devoted considerably to research. The amount of course work done in the special area would vary considerably in light of the previous study and experience of the student. It would in all cases be a minimum of one year's work or the equivalent.

Research

The development of high competence in research design, in the conduct of research, and in the planning and utilization of research would be a feature of the program. The research would be concentrated on problems of administration and related matters. During the first year, both in the core and in specialization, emphasis would be placed upon the development of knowledge of the contributions which have been made through research. The second year would emphasize basic knowledges and skills essential in planning and conducting outstanding research. The research emphasis would be culminated through intensive application in the third or fourth year—which would be largely devoted to research—under the direction of the core staff in cooperation with the specialists from the various fields or areas of administration. The foreign students and some of those from the United States would be expected to conduct their research on problems pertaining to education and related services in the newly developing countries. It is anticipated that most of the students would be engaged in comprehensive group research projects rather than in individual research.

The emphasis upon research is not intended to produce a research worker. However, a very large number of administrative problems should be attacked through the application of the scientific method. The administrator needs therefore to be thoroughly familiar with the importance, potentialities, and types of research. His knowledge and ability in research need to go far beyond the mastery of some particular research technique. It should take the form of broad familiarity and appreciation of ranges of research procedures. This ability may well involve high competence in some research techniques as one of its bases. The view that high competence in research is not compatible with outstanding administrative competence is rejected, though it is recognized that one does not insure the other. The rigor of the research approach need not dim the ability to work with and lead others. In fact, for many administrators it may be one of the imperatives for leadership—along with basic values, vision, erudition, professional commitment, and human skills.

Internship or Directed Experience

It is proposed that there be three types of internship experience. The first of these would be a general education internship for those interested in educational leadership who have had no previous experience in a school other than as a student. This should be designed to provide a wide variety of experiences with limited time devoted to any one specific area. It would provide opportunity to gain those knowledges and understandings which the teacher would generally get through his teaching experience. The student would move from one of these experiences to another when he felt he had gotten an adequate understanding of it. Similar appropriate experiences would be provided for those preparing for administrative leadership in areas other than education.

A second type of directed experience would be related to other aspects of the program. It would provide experience in working with others, taking leadership of the group in various situations, working as a member of a research group. This would be carried on through both the core and the specialized segments of the program. It would be designed to stimulate the development of the human skills which are so essential for the administrator.

The third and most important type of directed experience would be that following the completion of the formal program.

117

It would extend over one or two years. During this period the student would be a full-time special employee of a school system or other public agency with responsibility for a research or in-service development project. He would continue to be under the supervision of the staff of the program and would return to the campus for seminars.

THE STAFF

The project described would need a special staff, the members of which would devote full time to the project. The efforts of the special staff would be aided by an advisory committee composed of representatives of the university faculty and of leading public administrators. The special staff would be assisted in the teaching responsibilities by university faculty members from the specialized service areas represented in the program and from closely related areas. They would devote part time to the program in an advisory capacity to the students as well as in instruction.

The special staff would consist of a director who had training and experience in educational administration. He would be assisted by three staff members who would be selected respectively from three of the behavioral sciences heavily involved in the core. In the second year a research design specialist and a member responsible for planning and directing area and field experience would be added. These six would devote their full time to the development of the program and to carrying it through.

In conclusion it should be noted that the success of the program would be greatly affected by the quality of men who enter it as well as by the competency of the special staff selected to direct it. Adequate funds should be provided to attract the quality of student needed, and rigorous screening would be necessary. Without these conditions it would fail to attract "a few of the ablest minds" who upon graduation from our colleges and universities have many opportunities for graduate study today.

The variety of backgrounds of the students would be a major strength of the program. The diversity of the education and experience of the special staff and the concentration of the energies of this team upon a common objective—the development of administrators of extremely high competence—are also most promising. If the program were established in a few universities, an appreciable number of public administrators would be prepared in an outstanding manner to serve in the United States and in the newly developing countries. This is not seen as *the program* for the preparation of administrators but as one program which, if provided in a few universities, could attract and prepare men who would become leaders among administrators. Public administrators should be prepared through different types of programs. The resulting "mix" of men with different backgrounds and education is believed to be extremely desirable. The graduates of the proposed program with high leadership competence and research orientation should raise the quality of the "mix" substantially. The program might well also prove to be a leaven, as a result of which significant modifications would be made in existing programs for the preparation of public administrators.

Chapter VIII

Continuing Education for Present Administrators

Benjamin C. Willis
General Superintendent of Schools, Chicago, Illinois

As I considered the goal of new perspectives in training administrators and pondered over my contribution to it, I became convinced that although improving the pre-service preparation of future school administrators is vital, the in-service, or continuing, education of those men and women now holding responsible administrative positions is of even greater signfiicance at this moment. I say this because most of the major administrative posts in American education for the next 10 or 15 years at least will be held by persons who have completed their formal programs of education and who must learn in a variety of ways to cope with the problems they now face. The difficulty, of course, is that today we cannot accurately predict what the problems will be in a few years, since things move so rapidly these days.

We cannot consider either the in-service or pre-service problems of training administrators in a vacuum, however. Therefore, I would like to consider briefly some of the challenges with which these administrators will have to contend.

Obviously, the most dramatic challenge confronting us all is found in our international life. This is a two-fold challenge, involving both physical survival and ideological survival. At the moment Russia appears to be our major opponent, but in the end it may be that one of the little countries like Cambodia or Ghana or Bolivia will present the moral issue and the fateful challenge to our way of life. These are the countries which must leap from the jungle to the space age in one mighty jump, without the advantage of the evolutionary growth which we have had.

Recent evidence indicates that the Communist world is putting great stock in education as an instrument in the development of trained man power and is increasing educational opportunities at a much faster rate than is the Western world. Comparisons between the relative rate of increase in educational opportunities in those countries behind the Iron Curtain and those of the Western world provide cause for serious concern.

The implications for our school administrators, indeed for our entire society, are obvious. That we must become intimately acquainted with foreign cultures, eastern as well as western, has become axiomatic in today's world. My own experience leads me to believe that foreign travel should be considered an integral part of the superintendent's professional responsibilities. This must, of course, be more than a sightseeing tour. To be useful, such travel must be purposeful. It must involve sitting with educational leaders from other countries in serious discussion of common and unique educational problems.

In addition to the obvious benefits of travel, we would also learn much by the simple process of reading educational journals from other countries. My guess is that with the exception of some professors of comparative education very few of us in the profession avail ourselves of this opportunity to acquire knowledge.

Knowledge of these other societies, however, will by no means be enough. With the international challenges to which I have alluded we cannot afford to tolerate the social and educational factors with which our educators must deal, but with which our total society shares concern. These factors promote problems such as the drop-outs, the inability of many talented youngsters to get to college for one reason or another, and the educational apathy characterizing children with neither consistent school experience nor understanding of its value. These are problems facing us today; they must be dealt with by present-day leaders. Such problems demand the strengthening of our educational structure and the extension of opportunity to more of our youth; in addition, they suggest that we must accelerate our educational aid to other nations of the Western world.

A second major challenge is to be found in science and technology. The sciences which have provided us with polio vaccine and transistors and space capsules, have also given us technological unemployment and the capability for self-extermination. As Henry Drummond said in the play *Inherit the Wind,* "All progress has its price." There is little doubt of our willingness to pay the price of scientific progress; there are some questions as to our capacity to do so. As James B. Conant points out in his book, *Slums and Suburbs,* the existence in the slums of our large cities of thousands of youth ages 16-21 who are both out-of-school and out-of-work is "social dynamite." This problem, and the many others resulting from technological progress and other factors, must be met today.

The implications of scientific progress for education are limitless. To combat technological unemployment, we need extensive retraining programs for adults. To prevent the further spread of such unemployment, we need basic technical training for increasing numbers of our young people. Above all we must transmit a knowledge of history, an appreciation of art and literature, and the psychological insights which will enable men to control not only their machines but themselves. In a very real sense this reflects a challenge by technology to other disciplines, for technology is challenging the dignity, rights, and worth of the individual, to say nothing of threatening his very existence.

Two additional challenges which must be met by the men and women now holding administrative positions are related—our population growth and the urbanization of the country. In some of the foreign travel which I have been fortunate enough to make, I have been appalled at the pitiful overcrowding in places such as Hong Kong, where refugees who are able to live on a roof are considered lucky. But I certainly do not have to go that far to become apprehensive about overcrowding. Increasing areas of Chicago suffer acutely from overcrowding.

With the promise of a national population of 225 million by 1975, we are told that our urban areas will double in size in these next 15 years. That is not very far away. I do not have any idea who the superintendent of schools of Chicago will be in 1975, but I am certain he is holding a significant position now; and I hope he is acquiring some understanding of the diverse forces at play in these metropolitan complexes. I hope also that he is aware of the problems created by the mobility of our people, of the forces which create or encourage delinquency, of the relationships between urban and suburban areas that are bound together in these complexes.

However, his awareness of these factors by 1975 is not, at the moment, my specific problem. My problem is how my associates and I can get the help we need now, for I am firmly convinced that if we fail to apply our creative genius to saving the large cities of America now, there will be no future for us to worry about. In the eight years I have spent in Chicago, our public school enrollment has increased by well over one hundred thousand, so that at present we have over one-half-million children in the Chicago schools alone. There are only 20 cities in America whose total population is larger than our school population.

The problems which Chicago has met and must continue to meet are not unique; they differ more in degree than in kind from those faced by other cities. All of the larger cities have found that many of their new residents have common characteristics. Most of the adults new to the city have few skills to market in a highly industrialized setting. Their children have not been prepared for the new environment in which they find themselves. Their homes lack books or any form of mental stimulation. Unused to a highly organized society, they are understandably bewildered by the size of institutions. These children with all of the impoverishment of their backgrounds are our children, and we cannot abdicate our responsibility to them and to society.

These few challenges which I have mentioned are symptomatic of the type of problems which must be dealt with both today and tomorrow. Thus they have implications both for pre-service preparation of future administrators and continuing education for those of us who must seek answers today. In addition, I think they illustrate that the level of technological complexity which characterizes our culture, along with the complexity of our present social organization, places a premium on a high capacity for adjustment to change and a capacity for innovation. Today's answers will not apply to tomorrow's problems, so we must find ways to develop critical mental qualities and individual characteristics which will serve our people in circumstances we cannot now even predict.

I am aware that the people reading this paper are quite conscious of these problems. However, I fear that a great many Americans, among them some of our fellow educators and school administrators, are not so aware of them as we would like and as the times demand.

I am also aware that these problems are by no means the domain of the school administrators. Our concerns are shared by many—city councilmen, mayors, members of planning boards, state legislatures and governors, members of Congress—indeed, all those involved in our political life. From the standpoint of the academic life, these problems have attracted the attention of the political scientists, the sociologists, the psychologists, the anthropologists, and other students of our culture.

This shared interest in mutual concerns suggests that we should seek opportunities and techniques for bringing all these interests together for periodic exchanges of insights and information that would be of value to all of us. For some time now, since the impetus to the study of administration given by the Cooperative Program in Educational Administration, the American Association of School Administrators, the University Council for Educational Administration, and other interested groups have been encouraging the interdisciplinary approach to the preparation of administrators. This is constructive, of course, since no one can argue against the prospective administrator's being well versed in economics, political science, sociology, psychology, and the humanities. But why should the opportunity to draw upon these fields stop when we receive our degrees and leave the campus?

I shall admit that we now use the professionals in related disciplines by employing them as consultants for special projects, or we listen to them now and then at a convention or a conference. But I would hope for some long-range planning for continual involvement of all of us in dealing with the problems we are facing, and I doubt if we can accomplish very much along such lines in a one or two day meeting.

As a beginning toward what I consider necessities of in-service or continuing education for administrators, I would like to see an effort made toward isolating some of these broad social and economic issues that trouble our teachers and administrators. These issues are having tremendous impact on all of our schools, indeed, on all of our society, and they must be faced. Admittedly they may have a different impact in Chicago than they have in Portland or Hartford or Pensacola, but basically they are the same problems.

If we could have, perhaps on a regional basis, a series of week-long work sessions involving school administrators, representatives from the offices of the mayors and the city managers, representatives from other governmental bodies concerned with these issues, and persons from the universities who have given some time and energy to studying them, we might be able to move faster toward some solutions. It might be that by utilizing some of the creative genius of those in the field of education, we could be of considerable help to others with different interests in the same problems.

Not only the solutions concern me, however. I would hope that through the work conference process itself all of our horizons might be broadened. In his recent book *Sketches from Life* Dean Acheson makes a statement that bothers me considerably, although I admit that there may be a germ of truth to it. Acheson says, in effect, that men of action do not have time to be reflective. The implications of this observation are quite pessimistic, yet it is perhaps true that most administrators are so pressed for time that the reflective thinking they need to do may of necessity be pushed far down the list of priorities. I would hope that the type of work conference on broad social issues that I have proposed might provide some opportunity for this mind stretching. If this need is as great as it appears to me, then perhaps the one week session I have mentioned would not begin to be enough. Perhaps a month is needed or periodic sessions, held twice a year for ten days. At this stage the details are not significant, but I think the problem is.

Along this line, permit me to comment on the Center for the Advanced Study of the Behavioral Sciences which Ralph W. Tyler directs in California. This center is a wonderful idea, and the scholars who are fortunate enough, and talented enough, to be selected undoubtedly benefit greatly and make many significant contributions to our knowledge. Is there any reason why a similar type of center could not be established where school administrators and professors could get together under conditions conducive to serious consideration of some of the problems facing our schools? If Dean Acheson is right about action and reflection, then we must do all we can to provide opportunities for such men to be reflective. Perhaps the staff college concept that is proposed by A. D. Albright in his paper is the most effective way of doing this.

Of course we can expect that the bulk of in-service education for administrators will continue to be carried on by universities through summer workshops and conferences. It appears to me that many of these programs would be improved if, instead of competing for students, several institutions would cooperate in offering such programs, and draw upon the individual strengths available in each institution. What is needed is unity without uniformity.

It should be apparent from what I have said that I would hope these programs would avoid a narrow and expedient approach to such topics as busses and bonds and some of the other day-to-day operating procedures and would deal instead with some of the broad economic and social issues confronting us. Keith Funston, President of the New York Stock Exchange, has remarked that the eighth wonder of the world is the American economy and the ninth is the American people's ignorance of it. I would predict considerable interest among school administrators in a carefully conceived program on economics involving some of the top economists in the nation or a given region.

You will note that I said "a carefully conceived program," for many in-service attempts fail through lack of sufficient planning. The obvious futility of bringing together a group of superintendents and then asking what problems they would like to talk about should need no elaboration, yet we know this still happens. I would suggest that when conferences are planned, universities should invite some outstanding superintendents for intensive pre-conference planning and should then seek the best talent in the country to staff the conferences. In general these conferences should probably be highly structured to achieve the best results.

127

This may be an expensive process, but as in most things, you get about what you pay for. I am not convinced that universities should feel that they must give course credits for all in-service activities, but this problem of credit is less simple than it might appear.

Nor am I convinced of the validity of the generally accepted notion that in-service opportunities for administrators must continue to be a summer activity. Years ago the summers did provide a breathing spell for those of us in the superintendency, but this is becoming less true each year. A number of my colleagues have indicated that July and August are among the busiest periods of the year because of getting ready for the opening of school, and it might be easier for some of these men to get away during other times of the year.

As the programs of preparation in most universities have recently been making increased use of professors from other disciplines, we have of course created new problems. We have seen increasing use of sociologists and psychologists and others in research related to education, but we have not as yet absorbed their terminology into our daily vocabulary. The communication gap between the professors and the practitioners, already wide in many places, will become even wider unless we can find some techniques for bridging this gap.

For some time now we have looked to research for answers to specific problems, and we have been encouraged to do this by the universities. Yet the present state of our research in many problem areas is a long way from providing specific answers, and undoubtedly there should be some basic research in education which does not aim at providing answers now. Assuming that this is so, we need more understanding among all aspects of our profession as to what research can and cannot do for us, and I hope for some movement in that direction soon.

Although most of the concerns I have expressed so far have been directed toward providing opportunities for the upgrading of those men and women now holding administrative positions, I think there may be some opportunities for coordinating pre-service and in-service education more closely than is generally the case now.[1] For example, in Chicago we are interested in establishing cooperative relationships with a number of major universities all over the country to organize internship opportunities in our school system. With our decentralized pattern of 21 district offices we have many opportunities to provide prospective administrators with a variety of supervised experiences. It seems to me that as this program gets into operation it may be possible occasionally to utilize some of the advanced interns in an apprentice relationship, in the sense of having them assume major responsibility for some significant administrative duties. By doing this, we might be able to send some of our permanent staff members back to the campus for a quarter or semester, so that in effect we would be exchanging with the university. Obviously this would not work with all interns, but I do think we should be alert to such opportunities.

This concept of occasionally exchanging personnel might well be extended to other possibilities as well. The teacher exchange program between America and other nations appears to have been quite successful; some systems in various parts of our country have also exchanged teachers. It would appear possible to do some of this on the administrative level with the hope that some cross-fertilization of promising practices might occur. For example, if Chicago could exchange, for one year, one of its top central office men with someone holding a similar position in Detroit or San Francisco or some other major city, both systems should benefit in the long run by first-hand awareness of how different systems approach similar problems.

The concerns which I have been expressing for continuing education of our present administrators are real concerns to me, since these are the people who will be controlling the destiny of American education for some years to come. As president of the American Association of School Administrators I have recently appointed a nine-member commission to spend two years preparing a book on this subject, with the expectation that this book can

---

[1] The 1960 A.A.S.A. Yearbook, *Professional Administrators for America's Schools,* and various publications of the Committee for the Advancement of School Administration, A.A.S.A., have emphasized this need and proposed possible methods of dealing with this problem.

contribute to in-service education what the 1960 AASA Yearbook, *Professional Administrators for America's Schools,* has contributed to pre-service preparation.

In all of this concern, however, we must remember that, in the final analysis, in-service education is an individual matter requiring individual motivation. As a profession we must establish and maintain a framework of high expectations to encourage high performance. The daily commitments and responsibilities which consume the time and energies of most administrators limit or eliminate time and energy for self-improvement, so that despite good intentions, many of us encounter considerable difficulty in setting time aside for efforts in these directions. Thus I suspect we need to build into our professional careers some conscious, long-range efforts toward professional growth rather than assuming that this is something to be added on outside the scope of normal affairs. This may require us to do some convincing of school board members of the value of such activity if we are thinking of more than sporadic efforts in this direction. The challenge is to provide for the maintenance of a productive dedication to well-conceived purposes and thus avoid allowing unforeseen events to continually sidetrack interest.

In the instructions given to those of us preparing these papers, we were asked to consider the problems involved in recruiting top talent into educational administration. In my concern for new perspectives in upgrading the men in the field, I have deliberately avoided this in the knowledge that some of the other writers would cover it. I am convinced that the present effort of the AASA toward higher standards is in itself a device which will tend toward the encouragement of those who are truly interested in accepting responsible administrative positions in our educational system. I believe that this concept has been very well stated by John W. Gardner:

> If one is concerned to bring into the leadership ranks of a profession or a class or a society the men best qualified to exercise that leadership, the sensible thing is to guard the door with rigorous selection procedures, rigorous procedures for testing ability, rigorous courses of preparation. And the purpose of the rigor is not simply to screen out the less able but to screen out the *less highly motivated.* The ones who get through will then be not only men of superior ability but men of superior

character. The very fact of their surmounting difficult obstacles will have accomplished a vitally important sorting out.

We must understand that high motivation is as precious a commodity as talent and that if we do not have a system which selects for this attribute as well as for talent we shall have to resign ourselves to a good deal of flabbiness in our leadership ranks. And we must recognize that one way of bringing highly motivated people to the top is to impose barriers which must be hurdled on the way to the top.[2]

In essence, then, we are confronted here with the dual challenges of preparing administrators for the future and of meeting the needs of those who will be with us for some time to come. Both problems must be met at once, as time is not on our side. With apologies for not knowing the author, I would like to quote a statement which I believe presents a challenge to each of us:

> Great nations rise and fall. People go from bondage to spiritual faith; from spiritual faith they go to liberty; from liberty they go to abundance; from abundance they go to selfishness; from selfishness they go to complacency; from complacency they go to apathy; from apathy they go to dependency; from dependency they return once again to bondage.

I leave it to you to perceive where we currently are in this sequence. As for myself, I have expressed my concerns. By bringing our intellectual integrity to bear upon the challenges of our time, and by meeting and mastering these challenges, we shall strive to improve the quality of our educational program by improving the competence, intellectual sensitivity, and aspirations of present and future administrators.

---

[2] John W. Gardner, *Excellence* (New York: Harper and Brothers, 1961), p. 100.

Chapter IX

An Administrative Staff College
for Education[1]

A. D. Albright
*Provost, University
of Kentucky*

One of the major problems, if not the major problem, of American education and its leadership is the fast and ubiquitous change in culture. This culture change has two principal dimensions: rate and direction.

The astute educational administrator can identify and differentiate varying rates of change within his own milieu as he examines various parts that make up the context—technology, social organization, economics, political structure, belief systems, aesthetics, language, education, and others. Moreover, because the various aspects of culture are linked together, change in one aspect generates changes in other aspects.

The differentiated change-rate is a basic source of many frictions and conflicts even in the most homogeneous societies. These frictions and conflicts are, of course, accentuated by the heterogeneity so characteristic of American society. Some of the rate variability is common knowledge. Not only do we know that technology is an irreversible process, but also we know that its rate of change, especially in America, is so rapid that we are victimized. By the time a new complex has been integrated into a workable system, it has an excellent prospect of obsolescence.

[1] John R. Proffitt, Graduate Fellow at the University of Michigan, Kenneth Saltzwedel, Graduate Assistant at the University of Kentucky, and John E. Barrows, Assistant Professor of Anthropology in the University of Kentucky helped in the preparation of this paper.

133

Social organization fails to keep pace. Political structure becomes dysfunctional, and we grope for remedial measures. We pass laws (sanctions) that are expected to give strength to custom which is no longer sanctioned. Belief systems are porously punctured, or if we are fortunate, "slits in the helmet" are narrowed to give necessary psychological comfort by restricting the range of vision. The educational administrator, groping for solutions to school problems, encounters these change-rates. They force a continuous rebalancing process to provide equilibrium in the school system. Thus, the administrative leader faces not only the problem of change alone but the seeming counter valences of consistency and stability that are necessary for maintenance of some continuity in program, organization, and other parts of the system.

The administrative leader in education may find some solace in the fact that some control of change can be exercised in the direction that change may take. Because culture change generally proceeds from the simple to the complex, sometimes an evolutionary quality is ascribed to it; that is, it will somehow arrive at a satisfactory, logical position over a period of time. But this view is an illusion. The administrative leader, and others who perform effective roles in directing culture change, usually aim at a consciously pre-determined position that they call their goal. If educational administrators are to perform a more vital role in the direction of present and coming culture change, more attention must be given to their function of goal-setting for themselves and of assisting others in goal-setting for education in relation to the culture it serves. But plausible goal-setting and realistic means-determination can hardly be done without some insightful understandings of culture and its dynamics. And though we may be continually bewildered, even fascinated at times, by the problems and prospects emerging from the process of accelerated transformation, we are nevertheless faced with the responsibility of comprehending our circumstances. Goal-setting cannot be done in education out of its cultural context, as though it were an isolate, and the cultural tolerances determine the rates at which goals can be approached, once firmed.

Frequently, the most important factor in direction, as in change-rate, is access to ideas and concepts of other people. Isolation is always a handicap in the long-run. Various groups choose to keep out others and their ideas for varying periods of time. The resulting backwardness of isolated groups relegates them to living in the past, in defensiveness, and to relying upon outworn experience and rustic knowledge. Examples of social isolation and restriction exist in modern day education and in some of its agencies. We find difficulty in maintaining a realistic focus on our culture and resort to "worshipping the form long after the function has disappeared." Even casual observation, however, would impress any interested person that an increasing number of administrative leaders and of those preparing educational administrators are seriously attempting to overcome professional isolation. Perhaps this movement stems from the realization that the linkages among various aspects of culture create certain common elements of administrative leadership, regardless of field.

If education, at all levels, is required to perform major roles in the culture dynamics of change-rate and direction (while maintaining appropriate consistency and stability), it must be personified by effective agents of change in its administrative leaders. Perhaps one of the most important roles of the administrative leader is that of an innovator. Many persons would argue that this is the central role for one who heads a school system, a college, or a university. Whatever the degree of importance granted, his effective behavior in the arduous task of innovation is a function of general compliance with certain principles which have stood empirical tests, if not in education, in other fields. These principles relate to the involvement of appropriate persons in the innovation process, the interpretation and dissemination of information, the identification of goals and purposes, the sources of resistance to change, the probable effects of specific change in related aspects of culture, the roles of the innovator and others in the process of change, the social-psychological functioning of groups, the effect of existing formal organization in the process, the informal structures, and the explicit values and beliefs of participants. These considerations and others are ingredients for the construction of models for administrative behavior. The experience of effective administrative leaders provides substantive data when systematized and integrated into the models.

Two factors are important to the school administrator who is to perform the role of the innovator. One is the perspective of education held by the educational administrator. There was a time—when our culture was fairly simple and less interdependent —when a perspective bounded by the lines and conditions of the local school district may have been serviceable. Today, however, such a limited perspective is inadequate. The generators of change are found repeatedly to be outside the local community or district, even outside a state. Many persons living within local communities or school districts are members of reference groups that are national in scope. Labor unions, agricultural bodies, industrial organizations, and church affiliations are examples of national groups that exercise a profound influence upon their local units and individual members. And interests range widely, from civil liberties to economic rewards to foreign aid to population control.

Furthermore, in the past decade education has been assigned a prominent part in national survival and has become a prime instrument of national policy. At the same time it became more vigorously and directly infused into international affairs and commitments. Changes in the international scene have induced changes nationally. The common long-standing goal of education "to transmit the culture" is incomplete and obsolescent, particularly when this goal is interpreted by a school as transmission of localized sub-culture. Today we need a national perspective of education with the embellishments of international relationships. Practicing administrators themselves report the need of a perspective for viewing more of the cultural and social entity. Such a perspective demands administrative leaders of the highest quality and the most competent resources available for in-service preparation on a national basis.

Perspective alone is not enough for the role of innovator. A second critical factor is the translation of the perspective into experimental designs and plans for the improvement of education, plans which the administrator would initiate and execute in his school system. Any sound experimental design includes the element of evaluation. Often, however, evaluation is designed in such a way that only the successes and not the failures become the source of further learning. The reasons for either success or failure are obscure. In such instances, we may be able to say that something worked or didn't work, but little has been added substantively to professional knowledge and preparation until the question of "why" has been answered. This matter of translating perspective into experimental design, the testing of design, the distillation of data and knowledge from the testing, and the revision of design and perspective is an earmark of a profession, and it must depend upon a joint undertaking between the practicing administrator and those preparing administrators.

Educational administration is a fledgling, emergent profession. One index to its youth is the somewhat amorphous boundary lines of knowledge used in preparing its practitioners. Better definitions and organization of appropriate knowledge are needed, and the gathering, systematizing, and consolidating of relevant data are essential. This need is, of course, part of a need recognized in many fields, many that have moved a considerable distance. "The development of systematic knowledge of human behavior . . . is a serious challenge."[2] How can this be met? The task can not with justice be assigned as the sole responsibility of those preparing administrators in formal programs. Such a responsibility calls for a shared effort with selected, experienced administrative leaders who can provide pertinent grist. Obviously, this job would require a prolonged and intensive period for work and an implementation of the principle of continuing preparation.

Education can hardly hope to perform effectively its panoramic tasks unless it attracts and keeps administrative leaders of the highest order. Expert administrators are the object of competition from business, industry, and government. They are difficult to replace once they are lost. They need to be challenged in order to avoid becoming complacent. The administrative leader seeks advancement within his profession, and through his profession. In order to assure that educational executives will be highly capable individuals, continuous or intermittent improvement

---

[2] T. Shibutani, *Society and Personality* (Prentice-Hall, Inc., Englewood Heights, New Jersey, 1961).

opportunities must be available for those already on the job, opportunities providing a sense of professional meaning and dignity. Improvement in the quality of practicing administrators is dependent upon opportunities for periodic training in substantial depth and comprehension, regardless of previous academic preparation.

A cursory examination of current in-service programs gives the impression that such programs are mostly of short duration and deal largely with technical or tactical aspects of the job. These provisions are important, but they only partially fulfill the professional demands of practicing administrators. Just what would fulfill the mounting professional in-service requirements of administrative leaders is not obvious, but it does seem feasible that some facility for experimentation be initiated in the United States so that new methodology, content, and organization could be tried out and developed. Though each major institution of higher education may claim this as its function, it is unlikely that any institution could marshall necessary resources, make essential adjustments readily enough, or provide the financial support needed, while it carries on its other regular tasks of preparing administrators. Even in the formal academic degree programs, many institutions face great difficulty now in securing services from other disciplines in training educational administrators. Not only is the financial factor a deterrent, but also the institutional structures, policies, and customs are often inhibitors. Should an institution have within itself the highest quality of disciplinary resources in the nation, considerable frustration could be expected in bringing these to bear directly and fully enough in the preparation program for administrators. Existing institutions could gain some guides from a single source of experimentation without the onus of financial and other sacrifices.

But what might such a facility be? Cultural *inventions* are few, and time periods between them are long. An oft-used means, however, is that of "cultural reinterpretation"—a process of identifying an existing form and assigning new meanings and adaptations to it for particular purposes, when the problems and functions to be met are essentially the same. Education has employed this means repeatedly, for example, the internship.

An examination of other professions reveals they have, in general, some of the same problems in professional development, and they have devised various forms for fulfilling this need.

A notable example is an Administrative Staff College for business and industrial executives established in 1948 at Henley-on-Thames in England.[3] In England also is a Hospital Administrative Staff College organized in 1951.[4] France has her *Ecole Nationale d' Administration,* and Canada also initiated one in 1954 in public administration for provincial governments.[5] A facility is operated in India much on the same plan as that of the College at Henley-on-Thames, but with a 25 per cent government subsidy. The Technical Assistance Administration of the United Nations has fostered and supported similar facilities in Brazil, in Argentina through the *Servicio de Asesoramiente y Estudios Tecnicos en Administracion Publica,* the *Escuela Superior de Administracion Publica* in Central America, and in six other countries.[6] The United States military services operate five staff colleges for officer development.[7] Some of the professions and other bodies in America have also organized similar forms to cope with problems of continued in-service professional development. None of these has apparently interfered with the historical mandates or functions of the colleges or universities providing professional training in the fields represented. Instead, some evidence exists to suggest that these adjuncts to basic professional preparation have contributed considerably in several ways to the vitality and advancement of regular academic training programs.

A summary of the foregoing premises follows:

---

[3] Marshall E. Dimock, "The Administrative Staff College: Executive Development in Government and Industry," *The American Political Science Review* (March, 1956), p. 167.

[4] A. C. Stuart-Clark, "The Hospital Administrative Staff College," *Public Administration,* London, Summer, 1952, pp. 183-184.

[5] Keith B. Callard, "Administrative Training in Canadian Governments," *The Institute of Public Administration of Canada: Proceedings of the Ninth Annual Conference,* Phillip T. Clark, editor, Toronto, 1957, p. 52.

[6] United Nations, Technical Assistance Administration, *Training in Public Administration,* New York, 1958, p. 44, pp. 39-40.

[7] John W. Masland, and Laurence I. Radway. *Soldiers and Scholars.* Princeton, Princeton University Press, 1957, pp. 416-417.

1. The vast and rapid transformations in American culture call for more complex and pervasive roles to be performed by administrative leaders in education, including the role of innovator.

2. The changing roles to be performed demand intermittent, if not continuous, in-service preparation for the practicing educational administrator of high promise.

3. The in-service preparation should provide the means for developing broader professional perspectives, for constructing models for administrative leadership behavior, for designing experimental plans of educational improvement, and for gathering, systematizing, and consolidating data and knowledge appropriate to the advancement of educational administration as a profession.

4. A facility is needed nationally for experimentation with in-service professional preparation for selected, experienced educational administrators.

5. Other professional sectors which have similar problems to those in education and have devised ways of coping with these problems are a plausible source upon which to draw, in part, in designing a facility for administrative leadership and executive development in education.

Accordingly, a facility is now descriptively proposed which, for convenience, is labelled an administrative staff college for education.

THE STAFF COLLEGE

Certain general features seem essential for effective functioning of the college:[8]

1. Clarity and specificity of objectives.
2. Mature and experienced administrators as students.
3. Specially tailored program, organization, and procedures to support objectives and to accommodate mature and experienced administrators.

---

[8] See "An Administrative Staff College Plan for Education, Government and Business," by John R. Proffitt, University of Michigan, April, 1961, and from a mimeographed report by the same author, "Establishment of an Administrative Staff College," November, 1960.

4. Latitudes and opportunities to maintain an appropriate distinctiveness of objectives, program, and orientation.
5. A pervasive climate of innovation, inquiry, and intellectual quest.
6. Location on, or adjacency to, a university campus in or near a metropolitan area to provide over-all intellectual stimulation, to facilitate the availability of physical, personnel, and material resources for program, and to gain the advantage of favorable housing, transportation, and urban events.
7. Adequacy of staff, facilities and funds. The program and clientele require staff members with unusual qualifications. Special facilities, such as a carefully selected library embracing books, films, exhibits, and other materials, are necessary. Firm and substantial financial resources are needed to support such a venture.

Purpose and Objectives

The over-all purpose of an administrative staff college is to provide a program of leadership development for top-level administrators of education. More specifically, the staff college would be designed to assist selected educational executives in:

1. Developing new concepts. (Ideas, value systems, theory.)
2. Thinking broadly, critically, analytically. (Principles, processes.)
3. Developing skills and inspiration for leadership. (Vision, know-how, relationships.)
4. Securing information, data, and knowledge about our culture and society and the functions of education. (New findings, research, concepts in the human sciences.)
5. Rising from the liimted orbits of current assignments and providing perspectives on important national and international issues, problems, and conditions. (Cultural awareness, sensitivity.)
6. Assessing the impacts of these issues, problems, and conditions upon the performance of their roles and those of education. (Forces, movements, influences.)

7. Appraising the impact of their roles upon the economy, society and culture. (Social effectiveness, evaluation.)
8. Contributing clinical data and knowledge from their experience toward the development of systematic professional knowledge. (Cases, policies, principles, critical incidents.)
9. Remaining in education for a full career. (Retention, dedication.)
10. Becoming better fitted for transfer and movement within education. (Mobility, advancement.)
11. Designing plans for experimentation toward the improvement of education in their school systems.
12. Realizing one of the greatest of all stimulants to leadership development—the incentive to try the challenging, to experiment.

CLIENTELE

One of the most distinctive features of a staff college is the nature of the students.

The student is in the so-called middle range of his career and is removed by a period of service, anywhere from a few years to a decade or more, from the preliminary or advanced academic training which he had either to qualify him for entry into service or, after entry, to fit him for the conventional tasks he has been called upon to perform. He has gained some kind of professional experience and has developed judgments in the application of his professional skills and knowledge.

The selection of trainees is of great significance. One factor, that of the career stage, has been mentioned, indicating an age range of roughly 35 to 50 years. If reliance can be placed upon several studies, even though the findings of each may not be conclusive, certain leads are indicated for the selection of students for the staff college. Apparently, rather strong relationships exist between numerous factors and leadership potential, factors such as personality, knowledge, family and social background, high school and college activities, use of mental tools, self- and other-understanding, goals and motivations, communication, health, and others. Some of these factors can be assessed by use of diagnostic tests, such as the Index of Adjustment and Values for certain personality characteristics. A medical school has developed an instrument for gathering and analyzing certain social and anthropographic data on individuals. The Check-list of Behavior can be useful in gaining information on the performance of educational administrators on the job, and other devices can be used to obtain other pertinent data. Some written data should be obtained from the prospective student himself, particularly pertaining to goals and motivations and the relationship of the staff college training to these factors. This device would also serve as an index of the student's ability to prepare written materials during his staff college program.

Extensive accounts of the prospective student's professional experience and training would be obtained, including reports from professors in institutions attended and professional colleagues outside the student's school system. Particular attention would be paid in these accounts to the professional movements of the student, the kinds of continuing preparation he had gained, and assessments of professional performance he had given.

An interview with the prospective student, and with other persons in the school system, could be made by a representative of a university preparation program in the area. These interviews, following a general schedule, covering some of the factors already mentioned, would then be reported to the staff college.

Another factor in the selection of a student would be an agreement on the part of his employing board to pay full salary for the student during his program, to provide a portion or all of his fees, and to guarantee the student a position upon his return at least equal in responsibility and prestige to that from which leave was granted. Each enrollee would be expected to return to his employing board upon completion of his program. In no case would the staff college serve as an employment, or reemployment agency. The staff college would furnish a report to the student's employing board, if requested, by the board, and to a university if requested by the student or the institution.

With the composite date on each applicant, the staff college would select 60 students for each of three, three-month long programs annually. Each enrollee would be a full-time resident student for the three months.

The character of the staff college program derives from the objectives of the college and the nature of the students. Though the educational program would have some flexibility, the core would be constituted by the following substantive areas:

Contemporary culture and society. The emphasis in this area would be upon movements, issues, problems, and conditions in various sectors, and the relationships of these to educational trends and development, covering such areas as (a) fine arts; (b) demographic changes; (c) urban development; (d) military trends; (e) health and welfare; (f) civil rights; (g) societal goals and public policy as scrutinized by ethical and religious principles; (h) America's international position and commitments; (i) transitions in value orientations and Western thought; (j) nationalism, underdeveloped areas, and "uncommitted" peoples; and (k) related topics.

Comparative administrative structures, organization, principles, and their functioning. The emphasis here would be upon theories of administration and their reflections in structural patterns existing within different institutions and agencies, in organizational arrangements, the underlying principles which support the theories and patterns, and the ways these work with reference to: (a) organization for goal-achievement—planning, research and development, operation, program services, management, evaluation; (b) interrelation of units; (c) decision-making processes; (d) administrative authority, juridical control, and accountability; and (e) administrative authority and its clientele, pressure groups, social structures, and support.

Administrative leadership. In this area, concepts, principles and findings, relying heavily on the human sciences, would be related to the position, functions, and roles of the educational administrator in relation to such matters as: (a) maintenance of institutional vitality; (b) human relations; (c) goal-setting; (d) the formulation and articulation of policy; (e) morale, personal growth and development; (f) innovation and educational change; (g) communication and interpretation; and (h) social effectiveness.

The objectives suggest two further phases of a staff college program. Since the students are highly selected and represent the most promising professional practitioners, these resources should be capitalized upon for the development of professional "wealth" generally. From each student the lessons of his professional experience should be evoked as a means of building needed professional data and knowledge. Accordingly, a part of the staff college program would emphasize the *development of written materials.* These materials would take the form of cases, critical incidents, insightful observations of phenomena concerning behavior. But these would not be just any cases, incidents, or observations from insignificant experience. They would be developed in relation to the concepts, principles, and problems identified and clarified from the three instructional areas of the program. The initial preparation of these materials would start shortly after the beginning of the three-month period and then continue through most of the remaining days.

The remaining phase of the program would focus upon the *construction of an experimental design or model* by each student which he would propose to test out clinically in his school system. The design would center upon administrative leadership he would propose to initiate in reference to some aspect of the educational enterprise in his school district or districts, and the design would embrace and be built around the concepts, principles, and problems emergent from the instructional areas. Through the subsequent testing of these designs, some new and expanded professional data and knowledge could be gained and additional materials developed. Perhaps this suggests that some continuing contact be maintained over a period of time with the enrollees in each training group beyond the period spent in the staff college. Such contact might be established through institutions of higher education offering advanced programs in educational administration, such as those which constitute the UCEA.

The construction of an experimental model would serve as a vehicle for relating a personal philosophy of administration, professional perspective, relevant data, and principles, as well as a plan for the exercise of administrative leadership and for the development of further professional knowledge. This would represent a way for each student to integrate his staff college training and continue a significant contribution to the development of his profession.

Each of the three instructional areas would make abundant use of consultant-lecturers chosen nationally for their special knowledge and competence in the topics or fields to be covered. In some cases, international figures would be selected.

In instructional Area 1, these resource persons would represent a wide range of fields and affiliations—Federal government, metropolitan planning bodies, international organizations, independent associations, and universities. In instances, analysts and writers in philosophy, humanities, religion, and the human sciences would serve. At times, instead of individuals, films would be employed, such as the series "The Search for America," or Toynbee's recent historical titles.

Instructional Area 2 would use resource persons also, but they would deal with aspects of administration, such as those indicated previously. Recognized administrators of various institutions or organizations, "students" of general administration, and leading professors of educational administration would serve as consultant-lecturers.

Reliance for instruction in Area 3 would be placed upon nationally recognized individuals in educational administration and the human sciences.

The major presentations of these individuals would be made to the full staff college contingent of 60 trainees. Following these instructional presentations the 60 students would divide into six groups, or councils, of ten members with a staff leader. These councils would be expected to identify and clarify for themselves the major meanings, issues, problems, and principles raised and their pertinence for education and its leadership.

Various methods would be used for this purpose. For example, upon occasion members of the councils would perform simulated roles, either within the council or with the total complement, that portrayed a possible application of a problem or principle in an educational organization within a community. Council discussions, individual reports by members who took special assignments, recordings, case study analyses, and other means would be used in the councils to sharpen and deepen insights

146

and understandings pertaining to the three areas. Inter-council debates, practicums, and symposia would be arranged also.

The councils, under the direction of a staff college "faculty" member, would begin early in the three-month period to extract the lessons of their members' experience and to develop written materials in such forms as case studies, critical incidents, and situations related to the instructional and council concerns. As the instructional areas progressed, these materials would be revised in the light of "new" data, principles, and understandings.

Beginning midway through the third instructional area, each trainee would start to develop an experimental design to initiate leadership in his home setting after leaving the staff college. This design should be completed in time for consideration in sessions of the council, and in particular cases, presentations would be made to the entire staff college body.

Further planning of a program and procedures, which have only been briefly sketched here, should also acknowledge some other desirable emphases:

1. Time and encouragement for personal reflection, independent study and reading.
2. No degrees, tests, or competitive grades given.
3. Extensive informal mingling of students and staff.
4. A policy of maximizing conditions for self-awareness.

STAFFING

Adequate personnel in number, competencies, and skills must be provided. Salaries, working conditions, college policies, and prestige are involved, as are staff services and the procurement of resource personnel as consultant-lecturers, a part of staffing already mentioned.

Full-time personnel should include an executive director, or dean, an associate director, two departmental directors (program, services), a faculty leader for each council, a librarian and materials resource person, and a bursar-recorder. Sufficient secretarial and clerical personnel are necessary.

The staff college's dean, or director must be a highly competent executive, in addition to being an able and flexible

147

educator. The other administrative personnel must likewise be distinctly capable. The manner in which they function will quickly shape and re-shape the image of the college in many eyes. "The distinguishing feature of a successful administrative leader . . . is not his expertness as a specialist but his competence as an administrator." And further, "It is rather that the successful general administrator achieves eminence through his capacity to generalize, not because of any technical competence he may possess."[9]

Perhaps the key to the program's success lies most heavily with the council leaders. Each of these men should be an administrative generalist, while at the same time being familiar with at least one area of administration or with a closely related field. They should be drawn, probably on a rotating basis, from the top professors of administration in all areas of endeavor.

The council leaders, moreover, must have a particularly keen grasp of the factors and principles of effective group functioning and be skilled in their employment. He should be an effective lecturer, possess intellectual curiosity, and have an open-minded and flexible approach to his responsibilities. He should not be allowed to over-indulge in research or consultative activities, although nominal opportunity for these should be afforded.

The council leaders with a program director would be responsible together for the detailed planning of program and scheduling in addition to their council and other work, including frequent conferences with individual trainees in the development of their written materials and their experimental designs.

The staff should be employed and at work from nine months to a year before the first 60 students begin their program.

Under the Auspices of the UCEA

The UCEA would seem to be a logical organization for the establishment and operation of the administrative staff college. The UCEA is a "going concern." It represents leading institutions individually preparing administrators whose resources could contribute greatly to the facility; it has able and well recognized

---

[9] Roscoe C. Martin, "Administrative Leadership in Government," *Public Administration,* London (Autumn, 1955), p. 281.

leadership; and the staff college would be a vehicle by which some of the purposes of UCEA could be achieved.

The proposition is offered then that the UCEA plan and establish the administrative staff college for education for an experimental period of five years. Near the end of this period a comprehensive appraisal can be made to determine the feasibility of continuance for another similar time span.

Some thought and planning would obviously be required on several matters before launching. One is the establishment of appropriate working relationships with the professional bodies of educational administrators and other agencies. Suitable physical facilities and equipment would need to be provided, and the nature of the staff college suggests that the conventional provisions in most universities would hardly be considered adequate. There is also the task of program formulation with greater clarity, as well as the specific manner of organizing the staff college.

The problem of financing, as in any enterprise, must be tackled. In the case of the staff college adequate financing means a large amount of funds. The cost per student would probably range between $2,500 and $3,600. Secure sources of funds are essential. The time, attention and energy of the staff cannot be dissipated by the specter of financial shortage. The finances of the college must be stable, and dependence mainly upon income from tuitions and subscriptions is a fetterlock. But there are undoubtedly sources from which the UCEA could elicit sufficient support.

In Conclusion

The proposal of an administrative staff college for education carries no naive implication that certain of its features are unobservable in some graduate programs in some institutions of higher learning scattered across the country. There are, however, some important inferential differences between the staff college and many graduate programs. The main variances seem observable in certain objectives of the staff college as proposed, in the nature of the student group, in perspective, in some areas of content and its organization, in some of the procedures, in staffing, and in the ways that practitioners can contribute directly

149

to the development of a profession nationally. But, more important, the staff college represents a means of combining those desirable features of formal graduate programs along with a number of others within a facility devoted to relieving an acute educational problem, that of career administrative leadership development with experienced educational administrators.

Perhaps the number to be reached by the staff college seems small for the need. But in five years 900 would be directly affected; in ten years, 1,800. Should these numbers appear diminutive in terms of the total number of administrators, the professional impact of 900 may be multiplied many times. And there is a growing job to be done by the individual universities in the continuing preparation of administrators.

The concept of an administrative staff college for education, distinctive in means and ends, is proposed to aid men (1) acquire an articulate conceptual foundation, increased professional knowledge and sophistication, and greater comprehension of their roles in society, (2) develop sharper sympathies and flexibilities, improved analytical skills, self-assurance, and a finer appreciation of the complexities of our culture and of the modern world.

Nolo contendere that greater competence is needed in administrative leadership. Education has become an enormous and highly complex activity in the United States. It has been required to assume more and more functions in an effort to cope with myriad problems of a vast, interdependent, highly complex society. The perplexities confronting education and its agent, the administrator, are of astounding dimensions. And all indications point to further expansion of education's role in response to public demand, making the process of education an even more complicated and diverse task. With these conditions prevailing, the United States can ill afford to overlook any prospect, which has promise of substantially improving the quality of its educational enterprise. In our present situation, it seems intelligent to design new institutions, processes, resources, and patterns of behavior in education that may enhance more rational guidance and direction to our cultural and social transformations. An administrative staff college for education, a facility for in-service training off-the-job, is one prospect.

Chapter X

New Perspectives: Implications for Program Change

JACK A. CULBERTSON
University Council for
Educational Adminstration

Even though the previous chapters were written by persons with differing academic and professional backgrounds, the views presented are more similar than dissimilar. General agreements among the writers are evident in a number of threads which run through the papers: candidates for administrative positions should be well educated generalists; current career patterns and recruitment procedures need re-examination; a multi-disciplinary approach to preparation is essential; a variety of instructional methods logically related to clearly defined goals is needed; field experiences must complement university learnings; and preparation for educational administration is a continuous process, and, therefore, must include in-service education.[1] This chapter will build on the above generalizations and will highlight some implications for program change.

ADMINISTRATORS AS PERCEPTIVE GENERALISTS

Shaping the character and the scope of every preparatory program is a set of educational goals. Sometimes relatively implicit and sometimes more explicit, these goals reflect the image of the administrator which a given program would produce. Defining the desired facets of the image is the most

---

[1] Not all writers took positions on all of the above generalizations. However, most of the writers who took a position on the generalizations expressed support for them.

fundamental of all acts in program development; the definition attained will and should affect every major aspect of preparation. How a desired image can shape such major aspects of program as recruitment, curriculum, and instructional methodology will be illustrated in the pages which follow.

The thesis is offered here that the ideal image of the administrator, now and in the foreseeable future, should be that of a perceptive generalist.[2] From this thesis an important question immediately arises; namely, what are the most salient characteristics of administrators who represent this ideal image? First and foremost, is a capacity to generalize perceptively about complex problems and to take the responsibility for decisions concerning these problems.[3] As the perceptive generalist chooses and influences choice, he implements the principle that the whole *is* greater than the sum of its parts. He is able to grasp intricate economic, social, and political factors which impinge upon educational choices.

In today's world, the "whole" of the administrative milieu is characterized by an increasing number of complex parts. In school districts, for example, there are scores of teaching, supervisory, and maintenance personnel with many differing skills and knowledges. Such persons are trained to achieve definite and prescribed purposes; and they tend to view problems in relation to these purposes. Such conditions pose problems, as Laski has noted, for those responsible for policy development and its execution.

> For special knowledge and the highly trained mind produce their own limitations which, in the realm of statesmanship, are of decisive importance. Expertise, it may be argued, sacrifices

---

[2] This concept and others presented in this chapter have been discussed by the writer in the UCEA report entitled: "Improving Preparatory Programs for Educational Administrators in the United States: Some Action Guides." Members responsible for the report were Roald Campbell, Jack Culbertson, Stephen Hencley, Daniel Griffiths, Van Miller, Henry Otto, Truman Pierce, and John Ramseyer.

[3] The perceptive generalist as defined here, tends to emphasize the intellectual aspects of administration. Since a central goal of graduate education is the development of conceptual and analytical abilities, the definition is intended to have a functional relationship to preparatory programs. A more comprehensive definition would necessarily encompass the "action" aspects of administration.

the insight of common sense to intensity of experience. It breeds an inability to accept new views from the very depth of its preoccupation with its own conclusions. It too often fails to see round its subject. It sees its results out of perspective by making them the center of relevance to which all other results must be related. . . .[4]

Perceptive generalists are able to see the interrelationships of values represented in different specializations; further, they help ensure that these values are weighed against broader social and educational goals.

As specializations have grown, so have organizations. Channels have lengthened, and communication problems have increased. Contacts between administrators and the administered have become less frequent and organizational life more impersonal. Thus, problems of human relationships and individual motivation in large-scale modern organizations pose special challenges to those who head these organizations. How can organizational goals be related effectively to individual aspirations? How can morale be fostered and maintained? How can the many different talents of individuals be constructively expressed through activities that are distinct and creative? How can the initiative of individuals be nourished in large-scale bureaucracies? The perceptive generalist has a capacity for blending diverse human talents and motivations into effective patterns of goal achievement.

Previous chapters have emphasized and re-emphasized that ours is a rapidly changing society. In today's world, the drama of educational change is a very exciting one with an ever-expanding cast of characters staged before an ever-enlarging audience: school populations proliferate and schools and school districts get larger; school finance and business management reach into state and federal governments; problems arising from depressed areas and slum environments bring school districts into new relationships with municipal governments; and curriculum is shaped increasingly by world-wide forces and even by orbiting satellites. If educational leaders are to play a stellar role in this unprecedented drama of change, those who occupy administrative positions will need breadth of vision and a

---

[4] Harold Laski, "Limitations of the Expert," *Harper's Monthly*, Vol. 162 (Dec., 1930; May, 1931), pp. 101-110.

generalist's orientation. Of particular significance will be the capacity to fashion appropriate relationships between the purposes of the schools and the ever-changing society they serve.

Intelligence is the most immediate earmark of the perceptive generalist. However, his thinking is not characterized by the pedantic tendencies and infinite analysis which typically interfere with or even prevent decisiveness; rather, he will be intelligent *and* decisive, a sophisticated analyst *and* a vigorous actor.

The perceptive generalist should not be seen as one who has a shallow knowledge about many things. Extensive knowledge of a teaching field or fields, buttressed by a liberal education, will likely have been his first specialization. However, his interests and strong motivation will lead him to a concern with educational values broader than those represented in a single specialization. His capacities to learn new fields of application quickly and to relate them to social and educational values will lead him to positions of educational leadership. In this process he will learn enough about the various specialists in school districts to communicate with them effectively and to understand their problems and perspectives.

All administrators from vice principals to large city superintendents need to be perceptive about problems that are complex and relationships that are intricate. However, as the size and complexity of an organization increases and its environment expands in scope, the capacity for constructive action which is based upon perceptive generalization becomes more and more crucial. Top administrators in large organizations must be especially gifted in this capacity. Since several years of experience are needed to enter such positions, the work place as well as the university must serve as a setting where those who have potential can develop and demonstrate in action the capacities of the perceptive generalist.

PATTERNS OF EARLIER RECRUITMENT

From the previous discussion, it follows that preparatory programs must attract students who are intelligent, well-educated, deeply committed to education, and capable of attaining the qualities of perceptive generalists. No challenge confronting those responsible for preparatory programs will be more crucial during the coming decades than the recruitment of such persons. Central to the challenge is the increasing competition for society's leadership and intellectual talents among those interested in the administration of governmental, corporate, scientific, and educational organizations.

During the next 20 years the age group from which the great proportion of society's leaders will come will remain relatively constant in number while our total population will increase by one third.[5] At the same time, the proportionate need for managers and executives is increasing in almost all of society's organizations. Unless more systematic and effective plans for recruiting school leaders are developed and implemented, public education will suffer while the scientific laboratories, the huge business corporations, the rapidly growing government complexes, and the ever-expanding medical, legal, and other professions will garner an even greater proportion of society's talent than they have in the past.

One can seek solutions to the problem in either of two directions. One approach is to devise more effective procedures for identifying and recruiting school leaders from the populations traditionally used. The other is to identify and recruit candidates from populations not presently used. In recent years there has been an expanding interest in the latter approach. It is being increasingly recognized that a policy of recruiting administrators only from among those who have had considerable professional experience eliminates many potential educational leaders from among more youthful populations.

Thus, the choice of whether or not to become a principal, as a general rule, is open to persons *only* after they become teachers; choice concerning the superintendency is open to persons *only* after teaching and administrative experience. If the total population of potential administrators were represented by a triangle, it could be said that administrators today are drawn mostly from those represented in the apex of the triangle, and

---

[5] N. B. Ryder, "Demography and Education," *Phi Delta Kappan* (June, 1960), Vol. XLI, no. 9, p. 379.

that the very much larger number represented at the base of the triangle is not actively and systematically considered through existing recruitment procedures. Obviously, much more effective mechanisms are needed both in university preparation and in professional experience to attract and to inspire talented youth to enter careers in school administration.

Of some pertinence is the fact that almost all of society's organizations are placing greater value upon youthfulness in administrators. This can be seen in those who head federal, state, and local units of government. It is also evident in many top appointments in business corporations in recent years. To be sure, the need in a period of great change to overcome more traditional ways of doing things may be partly responsible for the increasing trend toward youthfulness in leaders; however, a major factor back of the trend is an underlying pressure to compete more actively for leadership talent by drawing personnel from among more youthful populations than has been the case in the past.

How can younger candidates with the capacity to become perceptive generalists be recruited into preparatory programs? The most extreme approach would be to recruit from public school populations as the military academies do. By focusing upon talented high school seniors, these academies gain a tremendous advantage in competing for talent. Since they draw from the total pool of potential talent, they are able to attract candidates who are highly superior physically, socially, and intellectually. They are aided, of course, by a system of strong financial and other incentives.

Obviously, such a system in the preparation of school administrators would be a radical departure from the *status quo*. However, for the more adventuresome, the idea is worthy of consideration. With proper incentives and financial support, it could be useful in recruiting and preparing school administrators. To ensure success, the idea would have to be adapted to important traditions in preparation. It would seem necessary, for example, to conduct such a program within the regular university structure rather than in a separate institution or academy. Such an arrangement would allow preparation for administration

156

to be integrated with teacher preparation. Until research has clarified the relationship between teaching experience and administration, such an arrangement would seem more desirable than a completely independent program. Also, youthful candidates prepared for leadership positions could begin their professional experience in school districts much more feasibly after having met teacher certification requirements.

A less radical approach to recruiting from younger populations would be to focus upon college freshmen and sophomores. Rather than setting up a separate program in the university for candidates drawn from the high schools, those with outstanding leadership potential who have not yet passed the half-way mark in college would be encouraged to prepare for positions of educational leadership. Those responding to the challenge would first enter programs of teacher education and meet certification requirements for teaching. At the same time, an integration of work for teacher and administrator preparation, and undergraduate and graduate professional education would be sought. Under such an arrangement, candidates could obtain background work in the social sciences and in the humanities as a prelude to graduate work in school administration.

Still another recruitment pattern would be to identify potential administrators from among those completing teacher training programs. Decisions on candidates could be made with the assistance of public school personnel. When those with outstanding talent were identified, they could be encouraged to consider school administration as a career and to enter programs of preparation. For those attracted to administrative careers, special patterns could be developed to ensure an effective transition from teaching to administration. For example, candidates might be placed in selected districts in sufficient numbers to justify the creation and implementation of programs of leadership development at the same time that these candidates were gaining teaching experience. Joint university and school district resources could be used to enable younger candidates to obtain background experiences and knowledge necessary for positions of educational leadership. Such plans, if successful, would not only increase the supply of leadership talent for the schools; they would also undoubtedly help keep some superior personnel within the profession because of clearly defined and challenging career opportunities.

Finally, one other pattern for recruiting superior candidates from new populations would be to attract personnel from outside the teaching profession. Those who have recently received master's degrees in behavioral science disciplines, for example, might be a possible source from which administrative talent might be identified and recruited. The potential supply of superior candidates from such fields would undoubtedly be limited. However, superior candidates from outside the field of professional education could provide excellent subjects for testing the assumption that successful teaching is an important prerequisite for effective administration. Even though the assumption seems to be a reasonable one, it has never been tested through scientific investigation. Perhaps it is time that a scientific test be made.

In all the patterns noted above, the discussion to this point has focused upon recruiting superior candidates to enter programs of preparation. However, it should be made clear that the success of such programs would be dependent on whether or not personnel in school districts would select their graduates for actual administrative positions. For this reason, patterns for recruiting candidates into preparatory programs and patterns for recruiting persons for specific administrative positions should never be developed in isolation. Achieving an effective relationship between the two patterns would be especially important in implementing plans to attract talented persons from new populations into preparatory programs.

If insurmountable roadblocks developed which prevented candidates from making the transition from university preparation to positions of administrative responsibility, recruitment programs would fail. Of equal significance is the fact that an extremely important incentive in attracting talented individuals into programs would be an assurance that they could make the transition. To be sure candidates should expect to spend some years in teaching and in leadership development activities before they make the transition. However, candidates should have

158

reasonable opportunities to enter administrative positions after a period of apprenticeship.

Plans to ensure an appropriate transition period would inevitably require the cooperation of those leaders in universities and in school districts who were willing to experiment with new kinds of career patterns. Representative activities in which school and university personnel might join hands are: (a) designing programs to communicate to talented high school and college students the professional challenges inherent in positions of educational leadership; (b) developing criteria to identify personnel with outstanding leadership potential; (c) creating outstanding field experiences to complement university learnings; (d) implementing leadership development programs to pave the way from preparation to practice; (f) engaging in research to test the relation of teaching experience to administrative effectiveness.

An important dilemma faces those who would compete earlier and more effectively for society's leadership talent. If those in universities seek to recruit into preparatory programs only from among those who have already had teaching and/or administrative experience, the potential supply of candidates is much smaller than it needs to be. In addition, since these candidates are older, and have more economic responsibilities in the way of families, homes and insurance, it is much more difficult to attract them into preparatory programs than to attract younger persons.

On the other hand, if candidates are recruited from among high school and college students, their motivations are more subject to change, and they are still untested by experience. Thus, the likelihood that these persons will all enter administrative positions is not nearly so great as it is with personnel who are already teaching or administering. This means that it will be more expensive, from an immediate view, to recruit and prepare persons for leadership positions from among the younger populations than from the more experienced ones because of the likelihood of higher attrition rates. However, from a long-range view, such an approach can be seen as an investment. Even if a few score of leaders with outstanding potential are

159

attracted into educational leadership from among those who otherwise would enter other fields, the value both to the profession and to society would be incalculably great. The importance of designing recruitment patterns which will attract talented leaders cannot be over-emphasized; the finest programs are of little avail unless talented persons enter these programs.

A Multi-Disciplinary Approach to Preparation

If perceptive generalists are to be developed, curriculums will have to be carefully designed and rest on a broad base. In addition to technical learnings, programs will have to encompass content from the social sciences and the humanities if they are to make potential administrators more competent in perceptive generalization. However, to say that the social sciences and the humanities should be included in preparatory programs is not enough. Since the social sciences cover a wide expanse and the humanities have a long and rich history, the problem of relevance must be faced. Those responsible for changing preparatory programs must decide which content is more and which is less relevant to school administration. If content from the social sciences and the humanities is to find a permanent place in programs, a logical relationship between this content and the practice of administration will have to be demonstrated.

Some general guides for determining relevant content can be illustrated. The old saw that learning content and experience should affect behavior provides one important clue. What, in other words, are essential behaviors expressed by administrators? The following are central to administrative action: communicating with individuals, small and large groups; making and influencing decisions; building and maintaining morale; and initiating institutional changes. Of particular significance is the fact that administrators of all organizations engage in the above processes, regardless of the specific purposes which they are seeking to achieve.

Developing Perceptiveness About Administrative Process

The above behaviors are strongly influenced by the perceptions which administrators have of their administrative milieu. Percep-

160

tions in turn are dependent on the concepts used to give order and meaning to the complex events which surround them. Since many concepts from the social sciences deal with communication, decision-making, morale, and change, they can provide a content that is highly pertinent to the preparation of school administrators. Of equal significance is the fact that social scientists have done considerable research on the above processes. It is well known, for example, that students of public administration have investigated the political aspects of choice-making; that communication in many contexts has been studied by sociologists; that psychologists have examined the dynamics of morale in organization; and that social change has been investigated by anthropologists, among others. Thus, not only is social science content clearly relevant to the preparation of administrators; it also exists in amounts sufficient to add rigor and power to programs.

During the last decade there have been various attempts to synthesize and organize concepts and theory into bodies of knowledge which encompass each of the above processes. Such organized bodies of knowledge can provide sets of glasses, so to speak, which can help practicing and potential administrators comprehend process variables, and thereby, become more perceptive about the implications of these variables for administrative behavior.

Knowledge about the social sciences cannot provide complete guides for dealing with administrative processes. Moral issues face school leaders as they engage in these processes, and such issues transcend scientific theories. Thus, science can provide pertinent understandings through such concepts as "community power structure." However, it cannot give a complete answer to administrators about the manner or the extent to which they should manipulate the "power structure." Since administrators have the task of selecting means which are effective *and* moral, they frequently face value dilemmas in making decisions. Since many of these value dilemmas have been illuminated in great pieces of literature, the humanities offer pertinent and appropriate content. *The Prince,* by Machiavelli, for example, is a classic piece of literature which deals with basic questions related to ends and means in administration. Since the book presents an extreme view ably, it is capable of provoking systematic thought about a major issue in administration. Therefore, it can be used both as a stimulus and a source of content pertinent to administration.

Another example of an issue which frequently faces school administrators is that of compromise. This problem has been treated in many pieces of literature. In Plato's *Crito,* for example, the problem of compromise is treated in a penetrating fashion. This is done through a dramatic case study in which Socrates plays the central role. This literary work, which has a universal quality, is another example of content that is clearly relevant to the decision-making of present-day administrators.

Not that such literature could or should be forced into providing magic guides for resolving difficult choice situations. Nor should the examination of such literature be narrowly focused on a single issue. Rather, it should be used to assist potential administrators to identify and to think clearly about some very persistent issues which will face them frequently as they engage in administrative processes.

Developing an Awareness of Purposes and Policy

Administrators who head viable organizations must be concerned with much more than administrative processes; the policy and purposes toward which these processes are directed are of equal, if not greater significance. Content which illuminates substantive issues of policy provides further clues about learnings from the social sciences that are pertinent to the preparation of administrators. Equal educational opportunity, for example, has been an educational goal of long standing; however, its specific meaning and the operational policies to achieve it change as knowledge about social and psychological variables increases. Thus, the phrase, "separate but equal" had different meanings in 1896 in the eyes of the courts than it had in 1954. These different meanings resulted in part from knowledge developed by social scientists about the conditions which surrounded equal educational opportunity.

The need for understanding societal trends and for assessing the implications of these trends for educational policy can be illustrated further. For example, what implications do automation and our changing occupational structure have for educational policy in regard to the following: vocational education, adult education, relationship of general and specialized learnings, job retraining, administration of school systems, and automated learning? Certainly such disciplines as economics, sociology, political science, and psychology have content which would be useful in defining policy alternatives in regard to the above problems. Knowledge about race relations, governmental relationships, population growth and mobility, urban problems, and many related phenomena have important implications for those interested in purpose and policy.

Knowledge about substantive issues of policy is not nearly so well organized as that which relates to communication, decision-making, and other processes noted above. A major challenge facing those responsible for preparing administrators is to see that content related to educational policy is organized in a more pertinent and concise fashion. A clear-cut definition and identification of substantive policy issues must first be achieved. Then, available concepts and pertinent research can be economically organized, and additional research on policy issues can be encouraged.

In his important role of helping set educational goals and policy, the school administrator is necessarily concerned with important value questions. The social sciences, of course, can help describe and delineate actual values. However, they cannot prescribe the specific values and policies which should guide educational administrators. Values, in this sense, are dealt with most extensively, not in the sciences, but in the humanities. Here, then, is another important and relevant source for educating school administrators. More specific criteria for determining relevant content can again be illustrated.

Today it is fashionable to talk about "excellence" in education. As a usual rule, however, the explicit meaning of the term is not made clear. A clear and comprehensive definition depends upon the answers to fundamental questions about mankind's highest purposes. Is man's supreme purpose the pursuit of happiness? Is it the pursuit of wisdom? Is it to serve one's fellow man? Or, is it for some other purpose? Excellence ultimately relates to some desired image of the "good" man or the "good" society. Since age-old as well as modern concepts of the "good" man and the "good" society have been dealt with in literature and philosophy, these fields of learning offer content pertinent to the preparation of administrators.

It is only a short step from the question of man's supreme purpose to that of education's supreme purpose, a question which continually faces those who would provide educational leadership. It is a question that has had continuous re-examination in American education. One of the last reports of the Educational Policies Commission,[6] for example, in defining the essential goal of the school, emphasized that "the development of every student's rational powers must be recognized as centrally important." However, as Brameld has noted, the implementation of a program for developing rational powers in students involves a facing of still deeper issues. In reacting to the statement by the Commission, Brameld wrote:[7]

> . . . any treatment of rational powers presupposes deep seated assumptions of a philosophic nature. Everyone or almost everyone, would agree that education should concern itself centrally with the development of rationality but this agreement is deceptive and dangerous until it is subjected to rigorous analysis of what the term means. For example, Robert M. Hutchins would doubtless welcome many of your statements, but he would interpret them according to his own neo-Aristotelian, perennialist conception of what rational means. Equally, a follower of John Dewey would applaud much of your plea for the development of rational powers, but he would mean by this something radically different from what Hutchins means. For a Dewey progressivist, rational powers at their best are equated with intelligent action manifested in the processes of scientific inquiry. For a Hutchins perennialist, rational powers at their best are equated with the capacity to conceive and define self-evident principles. All of these terms presuppose, of course, a whole body of assumptions about the nature of human nature and thought.

---

[6] Educational Policies Commission, *The Central Purposes of American Education* (Washington, D. C.: The Commission, 1961).
[7] Theodore Brameld, "What is the Central Purpose of American Education," *Phi Delta Kappan* (October, 1961), Vol. XLIII, No. 1, pp. 10-11.

The statement by Brameld highlights the relevance of philosophy in the preparation of school leaders. In a pluralistic culture, such as our own, school administrators need defined values about educational purposes and their relation to societal needs. Such values form a solid base for giving operational definitions to such terms as "excellence" and "quality" in education.

Developing Broader Understandings of Technical Functions

Another criterion of relevance stems from the fact that social science content can shed light on the technical aspects of administration. School finance, for example, can be taught in such a way that a bridge is built to such disciplines as economics and public finance. Or, an investigation of school housing can lead to the study of city planning, while school-community relations can end in an assessment of concepts in political science. Since technical information becomes obsolescent quickly, there is reason for preparatory programs to develop in administrators-to-be more general understandings in order that they may assess and utilize swiftly changing technologies more effectively.

Since social science content can illuminate the policy, process, and technical aspects of administration, its relevance and importance in the preparation of school administrators should be clear. As the social sciences mature, they should become as significant in the preparation of school administrators as the biological sciences have become in the preparation of physicians. Similarly, more systematic use can be made of the humanities in the preparation of school administrators. It is through them that proper consideration of enduring human values and the implication of these values for institutional goals can be achieved. As content from the social sciences and humanities are incorporated in preparatory programs, more careful consideration will have to be given to the relationship between undergraduate and graduate education and to the achievement of an effective integration of these two levels of preparation.

Appropriate Instructional Methodology

Implicit in the previous discussion were several basic objectives to be achieved in preparing administrators: (a) an understanding of and a capacity to deal with important administrative processes, (b) a knowledge which can contribute to wiser decisions about educational purpose and policy in a changing world, and (c) a broad understanding of such technical fields as school plant and school finance. Selecting content pertinent to the above goals is an essential aspect of program development. Of equal import is the creation and development of instructional methodologies which can achieve these goals.

Those in professional schools are responsible for teaching personnel not only to generalize perceptively, but also to act responsibly. Preparing persons both to know *and* to do poses special challenges to those preparing professionals. Two general avenues are open for meeting the challenge: (a) bringing the reality of administration into the classroom through such media as written cases, simulated situations, and filmed cases, and (b) sending students into actual administrative settings to carry out studies or to take responsible administrative action. The importance of providing opportunities in programs for responsibly and consistently testing concepts against the "facts of administrative life" is becoming increasingly clear.

Obviously, such traditional methods as lectures and guided reading can be very helpful in providing a base for understanding administrative processes, purposes, and technologies. Consequently, such methods should continue to have wide use in programs. However, it should be recognized that they are limited in their capacity for providing students opportunities to generalize perceptively about concrete problems, to engage in decision-making, and to take responsibility for implementing decisions. Therefore, lectures and guided reading need to be supplemented by approaches which do bring opportunities to potential administrators for choice and action.

Cases and Simulated Situations

Cases and simulated situations offer students unique opportunities for developing competence in perceptive generalization. They also offer opportunities for utilizing social science concepts as students practice skills essential to decision-making. Such practice can be gained without adversely affecting actual practice in school districts. Thus, providing opportunities for potential executives to gain experience in a simulated school is in one sense comparable to providing astronauts experience in simulated spaceships.

The Whitman Simulated School in the Jefferson Township, for example, has now been made available by the University Council for Educational Administration to more than three dozen universities.[8] In recreating the Whitman School, much information is provided through a variety of media: legal codes, board policy statements, staff handbooks, credentials of personnel, and many other kinds of written materials. In addition, actual people and events in the school and community are presented through filmstrips, tape recordings, kinescopes, and movies. With such extensive materials, ample opportunities are offered students for using psychological, sociological, political, and economic concepts as they make decisions concerning simulated administrative problems.[9] As they make decisions as Principal of the Whitman School, they are typically motivated to delve more deeply into theories of morale, communication, change, and choice in organizations.

Both the Whitman Simulated School and cases consistently present students problems in which value conflicts must be resolved. Such conflicts are sometimes highlighted in the materials themselves; at other times they become evident from differences in values reflected in class discussion. Through clearly identifying value dilemmas, greater understanding of conflict in administration can be developed and more effective means can be devised for coping with it. Since a series of representative problems from the Whitman Simulated School are programmed for decision-making, perceptiveness about a variety of relationships can be developed. In the pluralistic American culture, where there are built-in dilemmas arising from such opposing values as stability and change, cooperation and competition,

---

[8] These materials were created originally in the large-scale project directed by Daniel Griffiths and John Hemphill. See John Hemphill, Daniel Griffiths and Norman Frederiksen. *Administrative Performance and Personality* (Bureau of Publications, Teachers College, Columbia University, 1962).

[9] *Simulation in Administrative Training* (Columbus, Ohio: University Council for Educational Administration, May, 1960).

initiative and compliance, and central planning and local autonomy, the need for competence in dealing with conflict is clear.

Although cases have less background information and the decision situations are not so precisely structured as in the Whitman principalship and other simulated positions in the Jefferson Township, they do highlight many of the important variables which impinge upon choice-making. Therefore, they provide excellent opportunities for students to diagnose administrative situations and to gain experience in generalizing and making decisions about administrative problems. The long history of the case method in instructing executives in a variety of fields suggests something of its significance for preparing administrators.

Although the Whitman Simulated School and existing case materials are useful in providing students opportunities for generalizing about processes and technical functions, they do not provide students practice in gearing policy and educational purpose to a changing society. In other words, the decisions which have so far been simulated are management rather than leadership oriented.

Innovations in instructional materials are needed to provide students experiences with policy problems. Thus, long-range policy problems need to be simulated for instructional purposes. Desirable vocational education in large cities where automation continues its rapid advance is an example of such a policy problem. Adequate background materials could be simulated in relation to the contexts of three or four different secondary schools. Such materials could present important problems dramatically. Relevant concepts could be brought to their solution. Without such materials, there is a danger that their usual treatment in classrooms will remain abstract and even meaningless.

Certain kinds of technical learnings could also be simulated. Computer technology, for example, could be used to simulate scheduling problems in high school programs, the projection of school populations, and teacher procurement and placement in large city systems.

Industry has already shown the many possibilities for programming technical information in self-teaching devices.[10] Among the types of information which have been taught through self-teaching devices in industry are the following: introductory electricity, statistics, sales techniques, product information, and company organization. It seems clear that programming technical information for self-teaching devices is feasible in such areas as school finance and business management.

A major challenge for the future is the continued creation and evaluation of instructional materials. The development of cases and simulated materials, for example, will not only help to ensure a continuous supply of up-to-date materials; it can also contribute to the further growth of a body of organized concepts that have met tests of relevance. Those instructing school administrators must also take advantage of new knowledge and technology which come from the use of self-teaching devices and new developments in computer equipment.

School Districts as Learning Laboratories

It has been traditional to separate field experiences very sharply from university experiences. In the latter, it is frequently contended that one gains knowledge while skills are provided through the former. Such a sharp distinction of these two aspects of preparation is not justified. Although skill learnings are to a certain extent intuitive, concepts and understandings must necessarily accompany their acquisition. Thus, the general purpose of university education should be clearly related to the general purposes of field experiences. In the university, curriculum and instruction should be designed to assist administrators to generalize more perceptively about process, policy, and technology in educational organizations. Not only should students have opportunities to gain concepts which are basic to perceptive generalizations about administration; cases and simulated situations also must be provided against which to test and to relate these concepts. Field experiences should extend experiences for study. More important, they should provide

---

[10] American Management Association, *Revolution in Training: Programed Instruction in Industry* (New York: AMA, 1962).

opportunities for responsible administrative action based upon perceptive generalization.

School plant studies, for example, provide many opportunities for the application of technical knowledge. These opportunities range from the more technical tasks of projecting school population to the broader goal of using concepts about teaching, learning, and curriculum to develop educational specifications. Many other possibilities for organizing and applying technical knowledge can be found in such areas as district reorganization, school-business procedure, and personnel administration.

A myriad of situations offer opportunities for the study of administrative processes in educational organization. Examples of such studies are: the diagnosis of the communication systems of a given school unit; examination of the results of communication media used in a bond issue campaign; kinds of resistance shown by personnel to proposed changes; procedures through which administrators arrive at decisions; and personal and professional motivations displayed by selected personnel.

School districts also offer students outstanding opportunities for studying substantive issues related to policy. In many large cities, for example, there is the issue of whether or not members of minority races should be transported to schools in sections of the city outside their own neighborhoods. In 1961 in Chicago, for example, there was considerable pressure to transport Negro children from areas in which schools were apparently very crowded to areas where apparently there was less crowding. Such an issue would bear close study and examination, and it should be useful to administrators-to-be to have opportunities to formulate recommendations on such problems. There are countless other issues of substantive policy which could offer study experiences for those in preparatory programs.

Since schools and school districts are very complex phenomena, there are sound reasons for teams of investigators to undertake studies of administrative phenomena. It would seem desirable to involve teams of students from different disciplines in making large-scale studies. Representatives of different disciplines should be particularly effective in the study of organizational processes and substantive issues of policy. Another approach is for individuals to do studies on selected and more limited problems. The results of this approach could be cases, surveys, theses, or dissertations.

Internships, another significant part of preparation, must also be provided in school districts. It is in these experiences that trainees move into action. It is here that they meet or should meet the test of responsible action. It is here that the profession is faced with one of its most important challenges. The 1960 Commission of the American Association of School Administrators reported that those preparing administrators recognized the internship as the area of preparation where progress is most needed and at the same time where least progress is being made.[11]

Several objectives must be achieved if optimum internships are to be institutionalized as parts of preparation programs. A central consideration is having interns in situations where they can take significant responsibilities for educational problems. Routine tasks alone contribute neither to the making of perceptive generalists nor to needed experience in taking constructive actions. Consequently, school districts must be located which can provide interns significant responsibility; also those responsible for preparation must provide school districts with trainees capable of taking significant responsibilities and of learning from these responsibilities. The degree of responsibility taken by those doing "student teaching" must also be achieved by those preparing for administration.

Psychologists have clearly demonstrated that having experience is not enough. If learning is to result, experience must be understood and evaluated. Put differently, monitoring and feedback must be an essential aspect of effective internships. Both practitioners and professors will play an important role in the monitoring process and in helping interns obtain adequate bases for understanding their actions and for making needed corrections. The practitioner should be a model administrator himself who has the interest, time, and ability to provide interns feedback on the actual and/or potential results of their actions. Professors

---

[11] AASA YEARBOOK, *Professional Administrators for America's Schools* (Washington, D. C.: American Association of School Administrators, 1960), pp. 54-84.

must be skillful in assisting interns to diagnose their actions and the social systems in which actions take place. Those planning and supervising the education of interns will also see that they obtain representative experiences with the technical, process, and policy aspects of administration.

Finally, appropriate methods of financing internships are needed. The major responsibility for the adequate attainment of this goal will fall upon school districts and training institutions. School districts will have to avoid the error of exploiting students in the conduct of menial tasks to get "their money's worth;" they must view their central goal as that of educating future school leaders. Training institutions must view their responsibilities as larger than that of providing some financial help to interns; of even greater significance is the provision of skilled personnel to supervise internship programs and ensuring that these personnel have adequate time to do the task.

By way of general summary, then, there are significant and far-reaching challenges facing those preparing administrators. These challenges relate to such major aspects of program as defining the ideal image of administrators, achieving new recruitment patterns, determining relevant content in curriculum, and devising effective instructional materials and methods.

It also seems clear that preparing persons for positions of educational leadership cannot be completed in two or three years of formal preparation. Since administration is a complex phenomenon illuminated by many disciplines, in-service education must supplement and complement pre-service education. The need for in-service education is also reinforced by the tendency for knowledge to become rapidly obsolescent in the modern world. The point has been made by Morison in relation to the field of medicine:[12]

"This year's entering class of medical students are confronted by four times as much to learn as their teachers encountered a short twenty years ago. Not only this, but by the time these same boys finish their residencies eight or ten years from now, they really ought to return immediately to the basic sciences

---

[12] Robert Morison, "The Need for New Types of Excellence," *Daedalus* (Fall, 1961), p. 766.

they studied as freshmen. After all, there will be just as much that is new to them now as there was when they studied the basic sciences the first time."

Arguments to support the need for meeting the challenges of pre-service and in-service education would seem to be superfluous. For, after all, what one person in a school is more important in influencing educational results than is the principal? Or, what person has more potential for affecting the policies of a school system and its level of performance than does the school superintendent?